FRANCKSTRASSE 31

Gwendolyn Leick

Franckstrasse 31

Grey Suit Editions

The original German text, *Franckstraße 31. Raumprosa* was
published by Edition Korrespondenzen in Vienna, 2021

First published in English 2022 by Grey Suit Editions,
an affiliate of Phoenix Publishing House Ltd

English version by Gwendolyn Leick, Anthony Howell
and Dilys Bidewell

British Library Cataloguing in Publication Data
A C.I.P. catalogue record for this book is available
from the British Library

ISBN 978-1-903006-28-3

Designed and typeset in Monotype Bembo by Anvil
Photograph by Franz Hammerbacher:
Bannister Franckstrasse 31, 2021
Printed and bound in the United Kingdom
by Hobbs the Printers Ltd.

Grey Suit Editions
33 Holcombe Road, London N17 9AS
https://greysuiteditions.co.uk

Contents

Franckstrasse 31

The Street

THE AUSTRIAN CITY of Graz, second in size only to
Vienna, lacks the cultural glamour of Salzburg or
the impressive mountain backdrop of Innsbruck. Yet it
has geographical advantages that make for a beautiful
city: the river Mur flowing vigorously and broadly towards the south, a steep limestone rock, high enough to
build a castle on, which according to the local legend
was flung down by the devil. The finest buildings date
from the seventeenth century, when, as the Thirty Years
War raged, the city was the imperial capital of Inner
Austria, under Ferdinand II, Holy Roman Emperor,
who commissioned Italian artists and architects to embellish his native city. During the long years of peace
after the Napoleonic wars, Graz demolished its old
fortifications and the surrounding villages became
residential suburbs.

My mother, a native of the city, moved back to Graz
from the village where we lived with our father, after
my father's sudden death. She rented an apartment
in Franckstrasse, a street in the heart of the district of
Geidorf that was developed in the mid-nineteenth
century around the then newly built university. The
city proved an attractive destination for retired imperial

civil servants and officers, due to its comparatively mild climate, the absence of social disturbances caused by rapid industrialisation and the conservative outlook of most of the populace. Private developers purchased swathes of rural properties and built blocks of two-storey tenement houses on rectangular grids enclosing private gardens. The façades of these houses, or rather the thick layers of plaster that covered the brick walls, were meant to inspire confidence in traditional values and were thus fashioned according to the prevailing historicizing aesthetics of the time, favouring a bland interpretation of Renaissance canons. In keeping with the bourgeois character of the Geidorf district that grew up around the new university buildings, the streets were named after German and Austrian cultural heroes, such as Mozart, Beethoven, Schubert, Wagner, Goethe, Grillparzer, Herder and Humboldt.

Franckstrasse rises gradually from Grabenstrasse, an ancient thoroughfare leading out of the city, to an equally ancient road at the foot of the wooded Rosen-berg. The oldest building in Franckstrasse stands at the corner of Körblergasse. It is a small but handsome house with arcaded windows and it dates from the sev-enteenth century: it can hardly be counted as belong-ing to Franckstrasse – which had not existed back then. Franckstrasse, oriented from southwest to southeast, is sunnier than the streets that cross it at right-angles and it offers the friendly aspect of the Rosenberg as one walks uphill.

The street was not named after a poet or musician but after a popular mayor of the city in the 1860s, a certain Ritter von Franck, who had been responsible for turning the old fortification walls at the foot of the castle mount into a public park inspired by English gardens. He also set up soup kitchens, a communal savings bank and a public hospital; and these charitable works had earned him the sobriquet 'Father of the Workers'. I liked to stop at his life-sized marble statue placed in the park he had created, where he still stands in his frock-coat on a plinth, hands clasped behind his back, surveying passers-by with smiling benevolence. The sculptor had worked on the curls of his luxurious sideburns quite as assiduously as had Bernini on the Sun King's wig.

When my family moved to Franckstrasse, one autumn of the 1960s, most of the inhabitants were widowed women; there were also some students who had found lodgings in the spacious apartments occupied by the widows. There was not a single inn or eating-house in the street, and no shop; just a small tailoring workshop in a corner basement and one cigarette-vending machine. It was, like most of the neighbouring streets, essentially residential.

Franckstrasse was divided by transverse streets into three segments, of which the lowest best preserved its originally rural character because much of the space was taken up by the large garden belonging to the priests' retirement home. House number 31, where my mother rented a flat, is situated in the uppermost part, between Grillparzerstrasse and Körblergasse. Only the south-eastern side of this sector was terraced. One side remained empty until 1931, when the only plain and soberly modernist building in the street was built, a building which residents considered an ugly intruder on the Neo-Renaissance uniformity of the street.

If it were possible to render visible all the steps taken by a person in the city, the densest strand for my sister and me would be formed by the path we took, along Körblergasse and Goethestrasse, to the Ursuline convent where we went to school. Also the routes to the Rosenberg, to the nearby lido and to our friends, were concentrated in the uppermost segment of Franckstrasse. Walter Benjamin wrote of the formative influence that particular neighbourhoods may exert on a growing child and how the architecture and the arrangements of streets in his native Berlin had left lasting impressions. For me, having had to leave behind our previous life in the country, it was Geidorf that provided the backdrop to a growing awareness of the diverse modes of life, their constraints and conformity, that I needed to negotiate during these early years.

The Exterior

FRANCKSTRASSE 31 distinguished itself by the narrow space that set it apart from its neighbours on either side, so that the garden behind was partly visible from the street. This distance was perhaps meant to suggest the aloofness of a *palais* set in its own grounds. It was obviously a false impression because number 31, like all the more restrained and terraced neighbouring houses, was planned as a tenement, comprising of lettable apartments.

The building was commissioned by a certain Ferdinand Körösi, a person of private means, as it says in the documents of the Planning Department, who had purchased an empty plot of land with the intention of building a two-storey apartment house. He commissioned the then successful and well established city-architect and contractor Karl Walenta to draw up a design that would meet his expectations. In the application submitted on the second of September 1903, Walenta proposed that the building be accessed through an arcade leading to the *piano nobile* from the West, thus presenting a lateral side to the street, which was to be distinguished by a protruding rectangular bay. This proposal seems to have been rejected and other subsequent elevation drawings show a more conventional orientation towards the street and a symmetrical internal layout disposed around a central stairwell.

Although the planning department had curbed the seigneurial ambitions of the client, the architect endeavoured to satisfy his princely aspirations, especially in the design of the façades. They did not need to show the internal layout of the building in the way that modernist architects demanded, but rather hid the banal, commercial purpose behind a cladding of mortar and mouldings in such a way as to demonstrate the Körösi's superior taste and education. It also gave the architect an opportunity to show his own talent in satisfying his client by more or less skilful manipulation of architectural clichés.

The most conspicuous aspect of the house is the emphasis on the central vertical axis that protrudes vigorously from either side. A console bulging above the portal supports a two-storeyed rectangular bay and this protuberance continues into the attic storey, where a steep-wedged roof, covered with scaly terracotta tiles, thrusts long, spear-shaped cast-iron lightning conductors towards the sky. This splendid roof rises high above those of the neighbouring houses, and the bay, with its width of 180 m, overhangs the pavement and takes twice as much space as those to the nearby buildings.

This is less apparent on the drawings than in reality, as seen from the street. The high-angled central roof with its widely protruding dragon-headed down-spouts at the edges and the lanceolate lightning rods, as well as the leaded windows of the bay, evoke a late medieval and solidly Germanic ancestry. In contrast to this flamboyant central element, the lateral sides are consciously kept flat and restrained, the proportions of the windows and their pediments conforming in a simplified manner to established canons of Renaissance architecture. The strict articulation of this learned façade, however, concerns only the side facing the street. There is much more gaiety and a freer rhythm on the lateral sides – where alternatively arched or rectangular embrasures denote fake window openings clearly as such. A slightly projecting pilaster pretends to be a non-existing bay and the wall terminates at roof level in wave-like gables. This hints at the Baroque, and the cantilevered balcony with its stone vases has a decidedly Italian flair. In this way the building shows two attitudes, an ostentatious and ponderous German conservatism at the front and a more frivolous, southern playfulness at the sides.

The crowning glory, however, which must have been particularly expensive and thus cherished by the client, was the cast-iron double-leaved portal, two solid panels below, together with a glazed upper part protected by an intricately forged profusion of iron vegetation. Such a portal recalled a well-fortified stronghold and required considerable effort to push open. The

Russian occupation forces, so we were told again and again, were never able to overcome the resistance of this solid Germanic door. The master smith, who had here a chance to show his skill, was also commissioned to forge the banisters in a similar style, as well as the rosettes between the windows on the second storey, and the lightning rods and the geysers.

The exterior facing the garden at the back was devoid of decoration; here one could economize. Cheap wooden balconies, plain walls, simple window frames and ventilation niches had to suffice here.

During the time we lived there, the house differed from its neighbours also by the colour of its external walls, because they were painted in the so-called imperial yellow. This was a mixture of lime and ochre, which was generally reserved for public buildings in Austria, from Schloss Schönbrunn down to schools and post-offices. The rendering to this building, exposed on four sides to the elements, had to be expensively repaired at regular intervals. When we moved in, the plaster had deteriorated to such an extent that large patches had fallen off, revealing the brickwork underneath. A renovation of the exterior was therefore decreed, scaffolding put up, and thick layers of plaster hacked off. The nakedness of the building was now hidden by reed matting, behind which the labourers worked for months, alternatively pulling up buckets of mortar and bottles of beer. The inhabitants lived in darkened rooms, since they preferred to keep out the dust and avoid being exposed to the labourers' eyes.

For us teenagers the whole process and the fact that the house was under scaffolding was an interesting state of affairs. In the evening or at night we could clamber onto the scaffolding through a window so we could look at everything up close. The crumbling old plaster fell off at the slightest touch. We could see the pink bricks underneath, then the layers of fresh mortar and plaster. Eventually the painters arrived to apply several coats of imperial yellow, to blacken the iron-work, to apply brown gloss to the window frames. Then the scaffolding was dismantled and everything was as new. More than fifty years have passed since that time and several renovations have been necessary. For a while the house was as grey as its neighbours, but the latest, most recent restoration, restored its imperial yellow.

The Stairwell

HAVING ENTERED the house by pushing open the ornate pseudo-medieval iron door, the atmosphere inside the vestibule was lightened by a hint of modernity suggested by some Art Nouveau ornamentation along the walls. The glazed swing-door also showed the new spirit of the age in the asymmetrical curvature of its glazing. Behind the swing-door, a spacious stairwell gave access to the apartments and here Germanic probity reasserted itself in the leaded, coloured glass panels of the windows and especially in the wrought-iron balustrades forged by the same master of smithery who had been responsible for the portal and waterspouts; decidedly no convert to the *Jugenstil* aesthetic. The entrance doors to the apartments were set in wooden panelling, half glazed with opaque glass that allowed only a dim light into the hallways of the flats.

Every sound reverberated here; every step, every tapping of a cane, every word. We were always warned not to open the swing-door too brusquely, not to talk loudly when we went downstairs to the garden, never to yell, not to let the ball bounce, never to slam the doors leading to our flat, because every sound considered a nuisance, a distinct disturbance. In this way the stairwell disciplined the residents. Little brass knobs at regular intervals prevented attempts to slide down the beautiful mahogany stair rail; only at the very end, where some of the knobs were missing, was it possible to slide briefly and then to burst with élan through the swing-doors. The acoustic properties of the stairwell also diminished the opportunities for gossip, as any whispering could be heard clearly and was hence considered most unseemly. Intimate exchanges about other inhabitants had to take place behind closed doors.

There was no particular smell in the stairwell of Franckstrasse 31, quite unlike that of the house in Bergmanngasse, where my aunt lived. I can still smell that today – the smell of dog and schnitzel; our house only smelled of soapy water when the caretaker had done her weekly mopping of the stairs.

The stairwell served to connect the four landings while safeguarding the distance between the different social categories of the tenants, a distance maintained by emptiness and silence. It was not a space to linger in, just to get from the street to the flat or from the flat to the basement or vice versa. In what manner one mounted the stairs – swiftly or haltingly, proceeding with dignity or stomping impetuously, or taking several steps in one bound – all this was not just a matter of age and bodily condition but a matter of temperament, of conformity versus independence, of trying to demonstrate the dignity of one's status or to show one's disregard for it. Our father, whose nonchalant disdain for social convention I admired, had always taken stairs in bounds. He leapt over the regularity of any steps, whether going up or down; and his long legs could easily take three to four steps at a time. My last glimpse of him was him bounding down the wooden steps of our house in the country, wearing his white tennis shorts that showed his shapely legs, leaping over four steps at once.

The Mezzanine

THE GLAZED swing-doors gave onto the stairwell and the mezzanine, where two flats with identical floor plans were symmetrically disposed on either side of the door. Each flat consisted of three rooms, a hallway, a kitchen with adjacent pantry, and a toilet. Such flats were provided for people earning a regular if modest income, such as mid-ranking civil servants or shop-keepers.

While on the one hand it may have been an advantage only having to climb a single flight of steps, the fact that these flats were relatively close to the street meant that they were more exposed to the noise of passing traffic and to dust than the flats on the higher landings and hence their windows facing the streets were rarely opened.

When we first arrived, a brass plate with the intriguing name AZOLLA next to the mezzanine flat on the right made us children aware of the fact that people we never knew also lived in the house. When my sister and I returned from boarding school after a few months – my mother needed this time to arrange the move and settle in – we discovered that a Frau Azolla lived there and that the name was pronounced with the accent on the initial syllable. Because of her unusual name we imagined her as being herself unusual and were disappointed when we saw nothing remarkable – she was neither fat nor thin, neither tall nor short, no longer young but not yet terribly old. The widow of a civil servant, she was not well-off nor was she destitute. The most remarkable thing about Frau Azolla was the state of her nerves.

It was a heavy blow to the nervous Frau Azolla that three children under the age of ten now rampaged in the flat directly above hers. We came straight from the countryside, where we had been allowed considerable freedom, and our mother was not always able to restrain our vivacity. For Frau Azolla our trampling above and our screaming in the garden below were insufferable. When she had enough of our noisy quarrelling in the garden, she burst through her kitchen door, wildly brandishing a dust-cloth. Her nervous hair on end, she threateningly raised a fist before she slammed the kitchen door shut again. When the disturbance came from above, she tapped on the ceiling with a broomstick. If this failed she took recourse to the telephone: the word Azolla should have been enough. When even that failed to bring the desired calm she would ring our doorbell, begging my mother to curb the children's exuberance in view of her poor nerves. In general she liked my mother, felt sorry for her – so young, freshly widowed, unable to control these three brats of hers.

She sometimes gave my mother little gifts – flowers, fruit – which my sister and I were to fetch from her kitchen. We saw that she lived in a gloomy flat filled with dark pieces of furniture. There was a dining table in the centre of her living-room, where nobody had eaten for decades. On the wall hung a framed photograph of a man with his hair parted on one side, wearing glasses, apparently Herr Azolla. Should she have ever mentioned her husband to my mother, we never heard of it. As the years passed, there were fewer occasions to complain about the noise. She was able to leave the kitchen door open during the summer months and did not need to use her broomstick. At my mother's funeral she silently clasped my hand, her face wet with tears.

The flat opposite Fran Azolla's was not occupied until some months after we had moved in. We were at first pleased to hear that the new tenants were a woman with two boys of roughly the same age as me and my sister. Although the father of Mrs N. was a wealthy man with influence, who had managed to consolidate two thirds of the various titles of ownership in favour of his daughter, she found herself in the deplorable situation of having to live in one of the smaller apartments despite the fact that she was the majority owner because these larger flats were already occupied. At least it was agreed that the use of garden, originally restricted to the inhabitants of the first floor, should be equally shared between the two parties. My mother was glad of this arrangement as it meant that the maintenance of the garden, especially the mowing of the grass, would now also be shared. She thought that we children would make friends with the boys. This did not happen. We could not stand each other and we retreated to our respective sides of the garden or preferred not to go down when the boys were there.

Frau N. was of a similar age as my mother, in her mid-thirties. She was not a widow but a divorcée, a circumstance that made Frau Azolla side with my mother. None of the residents in this house owned a car. The tram stop was only a few minutes walk away and the city centre within easy walking distance. Frau N. used a bicycle to go to work as a secretary. She did not know how to comport herself towards my mother, a *Frau Doktor*, who had taken possession of the best apartment in the house. She preferred to stick her nose in the air whenever they came face to face on the stairs or on the street, thus making it clear that she didn't even notice my mother's existence.

I was only once in Frau N.'s flat. My brother had got drunk and vomited from the window, soiling Frau N.'s sill below. She rang the doorbell, loudly complaining about this insolence, the terrible mess. I took a bucket with water and some rags to clean it up. The flat was light and airy, quite different to the dark atmosphere in Frau Azolla's and showed itself in a much more friendly light than I had expected. I do not know whether Frau N.'s desire to live on the first floor was ever realized.

In the Basement

Below Frau Azolla's living-room window, on the western side of the front garden, was the entrance to the cellar. A wooden ramp led to the lowest parts of the building. Sacks of coal and firewood were dragged down this ramp and every other day the caretaker had to manoeuvre the large metal refuse containers for the municipal refuse collection. The caretaker was also responsible for keeping this cellar door locked as the tenants used the main stairwell to reach their dedicated cellar compartments where the coal was stored. Only a dim light penetrated into the cellar's interior from the outside and one had to turn on a single bare bulb to find one's way to the soot-blackened vaults.

Soon after we moved in my mother had central heating installed in the flat and so there no need to go to the cellar for coal or for wood. The house in the country where we used to live had had a low and vaulted cellar where the upholsterer, whose shop had been on the ground floor, kept a great heap of coal on one side and an equally great heap of sawdust on the other. We children would sometimes climb in through a porthole. The contrast between the hard coal that smelled of ancient earth and the fine dry sawdust that still smelled of the forest made it worthwhile crouching there in the dark. The cellar in the city held no such attraction.

There was also a lumber room for each tenant. Ours was fairly large; we kept the skis there, the sledge, our old doll's houses, the wooden cross for the Christmas tree and various old pieces of furniture. I disliked going into this place because the fat black spiders that jumped unpredictably in their dusty nets there always gave me the shivers.

At the time when the house was built, the washing of clothes and linen had to be done without electrical devices and parts of the basement were fitted out as laundry rooms. There was a walled-in copper kettle that could be heated from a fireplace underneath and vast stone basins that were reserved for rinsing. The hard work of washing was done by the housemaids or by specially commissioned washerwomen. I never saw anybody using this equipment; the rooms were abandoned and plaster was falling from walls that still harboured the damp.

Right next to the laundry was a small room that could have been used for ironing. The name Franziska Kranner was written in cursive letters on a piece of card tacked to the door of the smallest residential unit in the tenement. Not much sun came through the narrow single window into this room furnished with a single bed, a small wooden table, a wooden chair and a chest of drawers. It was just an ordinary mean little room and it could not account for the extraordinary strong smell that slipped under its door into the surrounding cellar compartments and which became almost overwhelming when the door was opened. My sister and I were familiar with this reek from the miserable hovels in which aged farm maids lived out their lives in the countryside. It was a miasma of never-washed bodies, dried urine, mouse droppings and mould. These old women with their headscarves drawn deeply over their eyes, their long threadbare and patched skirts, their humped backs and toothless mouths, carried the stink of their hovels in their rags so that they could be detected by their smell before they could be seen. We were afraid of these poor creatures because they looked just like the illustrations of witches in our storybooks and because they raised their sticks to threaten the children staring at them. Frau Kranner's room, in the most elaborately built house in Franckstrasse, in one of the most respectable neighbourhoods of the city, was a long way from the old farmsteads we had known in our country childhood. However, it still harboured something of the wildness and the freedom we had know there. The strong smell reminded us of our previous life and we did not find it repugnant.

Frau Kranner, leaning against the low stone wall that was just the right height for her, liked to watch us when we played or fought each other in the garden. She was always friendly and said hello when we greeted her. Sometimes she invited us to her room to offer us something – an apple for instance, which we never wanted to eat. By her window she had various jars, some filled with dandelion flowers. These yellow flowers, exposed to the sun, turned into a thick brown liquid which she drank with hot water to cure her cough. She never said much, hardly spoke at all, but apparently she had been born the illegitimate child of a farm maid and then she had left that farm at some point and come to the city where she had gone into service. Since her employers had died she lived here, contentedly, in this little room.

She was always pleased to show us her greatest treasure, a small blurred black-and-white photograph that showed an enormous pig from the side and next to it one could see the contours of a small person. That had been her, with that beautiful pig. It was hard to say if the photograph represented Frau Kranner as a child or a young woman because she was abnormally short of stature. She was the same size as I was at the age of nine, and therefore, among ourselves, we always called her the Little Woman. She was not a dwarf though – only severely stunted in her growth; she was sturdy, a bit stout, and her hands were large and red from all the hard work she had done: all the washing, sweeping, carrying, cleaning.

One summer a stray cat chose to live with her and she was happy when she stood by the window with the cat pressing against her. It was a shy cat which could not be touched by anyone else. By then we had got used to life in the city and took little notice of the Little Woman. One day a new smell emanated from her room, no longer reeking of ancient maids but of decay. The wife of the caretaker said that the stink and the flies were becoming unbearable. Since Frau Kranner did not answer when called, her door had to be broken by force. There she sat on her bed, cradling the long dead cat in her arms and the Little Woman resisted attempts to have the decaying animal taken from her with all her might. I don't remember whether the police or the fire brigade or some other authority decided that she could no longer continue to live at number 31. She was taken away and we never saw her again. And gradually we forgot about her.

The last thing we heard of the Little Woman was that she had been found sitting on a bench in the Rosenhain, one of the forested parks around Graz, sitting on a bench in the sun, quite peaceful and quite dead.

On the eastern side of the basement, separated from the cellar compartment by the stairwell, was the flat given over to a couple in exchange for caretaking duties. The terracing of the building towards the garden meant that this flat was level with the ground. The windows over-looked the modest enclosed area of grass that was accessible to all tenants for such purposes as the beating of carpets but the orientation towards the north and the shadow falling from the neighbouring building did not allow direct sunlight into its rooms. The flat did not have a bathroom and the toilet in the hallways was also used by the Little Woman.

From the time we moved in until the mid-1960s, it was inhabited by a family called Richter. The husband went to work each day. He could perform his caretaking duties on the side – to drag the metal refuse containers up the ramp for collection, to cut the grass of the collective spaces and to trim the hedges and flowers that grew there, to sweep the snow from the pavement, to spread ashes in front of the house in the winter and to unlock the front door to visitors arriving after dark. Herr Richter was a wiry man in his forties and quite without the sort of servility which the bourgeois residents were accustomed to expect. After all he was not someone working full-time rendering these services but a class-conscious worker. My mother said he was a prole and considered his refusal to address her as 'Frau Doktor' as an impudence typical for his class. He had a way of holding his head at an angle with a scrutinizing, even scornful look. He owned a moped – a proletarian vehicle, on which he made excursions to the sur-rounding mountains on weekends. In his rucksack he brought back different kinds of rocks that he assembled in the front garden, creating an Alpine garden where he cultivated various Alpine flowers. Gentians, wild orchids and valerian, even edelweiss thrived on this miniature mountain and were much admired by those who walked past on their Sunday constitutionals.

His wife took charge of the remaining caretaking duties: the sweeping and washing of the stairs and floors in the internal communal spaces, the dusting of the wrought-iron balustrade, the polishing of the mahogany guard rail and the brass knobs. She took care of the airing of the stairwell and made sure the windows were fastened during thunderstorms. These duties left her enough time for her own household and she was also prepared to assist certain tenants for an hourly rate. My mother would never have coped with the window-cleaning without Frau Richter, as they were too unwieldy and heavy for one person to handle. She was equally indispensable for the yearly spring-cleaning. For a while she came regularly to do the vacuuming but my mother found her strong body odour unbearable. Frau Richter always wore a button-through apron during the week and covered her greying hair with a scarf tied at the forehead. She was more used to deal with her betters than her husband, but was equally not prepared to be ordered about.

Their sons were apprenticed somewhere. A few years older than my sister and me, they ignored us. We rarely saw them, just caught glimpses of them tinkering with the moped or throwing darts at the cut-out faces of film stars pinned to the shed wall. They were not teddy boys, they did not riot, they were hardly at home, preferring the company of their peers. When they went out, they always used the cellar ramp through the front garden, never the stairwell. They wore tight trousers and slicked-back hair. The whole family spoke the urban working-class accent with which we were not familiar, quite different from the accent we knew from the countryside.

One day they all moved out. I don't know whether Herr Richter changed his work place or retired, nor do I know where they went. They dismantled the alpine garden, the only alpine garden in Franckstrasse, and carried away the rocks and plants. The owners of the building were no longer prepared to have anyone live rent-free in exchange for caretaking and preferred to let the flat to paying tenants. They installed an electric door-opening system and the various caretaking duties were contracted out to people who did not live there. As a result the last working-class residents disappeared from the house.

The Garden

THE FRONT GARDENS of the *fin-de-siècle* neighbour-hoods in Graz are said to be a particularly charming characteristic of the city. Enclosed by cast-iron fences, they form a green hiatus between pavement and build-ings. These front gardens irritated me as they were not proper gardens, first by being too small and then by being too public for anyone ever to make use of them. Due to a desire to conform, or because of a lack of imagination, they were always stocked with the same assortment of plants chosen for their longevity, weather-resistance and ease of care. Hydrangeas were by far the most popular choice, growing into dense sprawling bushes that produced pink or light blue flowers every year. These flowers did not fall off but clung to the leafless stalks, their colour faded or dark-ened in a suspended animation that persisted even into the depths of winter, defying frost and snow. Once a hydrangea was established in a front garden, other flowers and shrubs had little chance of surviving. It was hydrangeas that flourished in the front garden of Franckstrasse 31, which extended to the sides of the building, while the roses and badly pruned box trees made a poor show. After the caretaker's alpine garden disappeared there was no more reason to linger before this front garden.

Behind the house and situated at a lower level was a formally laid-out garden, bordering the fields belonging to the convent of the Sisters of the Cross. The original layout of the garden consisted of two grassed surfaces, equally divided by a central path, each containing two circular and two rectangular flower beds, while various shrubs screened the fences between the neighbouring gardens. The central path led to a terrace paved with flagstones, with two apple trees in front and two pear trees behind it. A wooden bench allowed the contemplation of the building's undistinguished rear façade. Fine fruit trees of the kind that flourished in the city's southern climate – apricots and peaches – had been planted at regular intervals between the rose beds. When we arrived, nearly sixty years after the garden had first been laid out, one could just about recognize the original design, although the symmetry had long been compromised, as the construction of the post-war building next door had led to a change of the eastern boundary.

The fruit trees had reached the end of their lifespan. They had been neglected during the war years and had died one after the other. The gravel paths along the outer perimeter were grassed over and hardly discernible. The wooden garden shed, overgrown with Virginia creeper, was about to collapse. The roses suffered from rust and perished. They were not replaced. Only the hardy tree peonies with their large serrated white petals flowered stoically every June.

The clause of the tenancy agreement that reserved the use of the whole garden for the occupants of the first floor flat had confirmed my mother's decision to rent the flat that had just become available. She wished to compensate us for the loss of freedom we had enjoyed in the country, where we had roamed the fields, meadows, streams and forests, by letting us have access to this garden. We were not exactly thrilled with the boring expanse of grass and the dying trees that this city garden offered. The only thing we liked was the swing suspended from a free-standing timber structure. With enough effort one could get as high as the topmost branches of the apricot tree to reach the ripest and juiciest of the fruit – until one day a bolt of lightning felled tree and swing in one blast.

A simple wire mesh fence separated the long east-to-west lying garden of the Sisters of the Cross from ours. This large area served to feed the nuns and it reminded us of the fields in the country, especially during the cold season when the field in the middle showed its brown, ploughed earth. It was easy to slip into that garden through a gap in the fence behind the shed. We were after the redcurrants and a particularly flavoursome variety of eating apple.

The gardens belonging to the neighbouring buildings on either side of ours were almost completely overgrown with trees and bushes that were never cut; they were dark and nobody ever went there. During the time the cherries were ripe we climbed one of the trees to steal the big, wormy but sweet cherries that nobody bothered to harvest.

My mother took no interest in the garden. She was too busy with the household to take on extra work and digging in the earth held no thrill for her, especially not under the eyes of the other tenants. She hardly ever went down there and although she could bask in the sun for hours she never did that in the Franckstrasse garden. After the new tenants had moved into the vacant flat on the mezzanine they insisted on sharing the use of the garden and we were assigned the eastern half with the garden shed.

When our brother, who was younger, started to attend a nursery school on the nearby Rosenberg, this park-like forest with its ancient beech tree became our favourite play area. There were duck ponds, trees one could climb, bushes to hide in and a mysterious enclosure said to have harboured wolves in the past. We were still sent to play in our garden but stayed there unwillingly, feeling too exposed to the resentful eyes of the tenants. We felt hemmed in, as in the horrible garden at the convent school, where we had to walk the gravelled paths in a crocodile, two by two.

Somebody gave me an Indian tepee. It was just about big enough for one crouching person but at least one could read there undisturbed. In the last year of my time in Franckstrasse I began to read Proust in the original, continually looking up vocabulary in the dictionary, again and again reading the long sentences from the beginning, sentences that escaped, that resisted, comprehension, but I was enthralled. Lying in the sun, head and shoulders in the tepee, I read the small-printed paperback edition of *Du Côté de chez Swann* for the first time. Whenever I think of Cambray it evokes the smell of squashed grass and of decaying, sun-heated canvas.

My mother began to bring various saplings from excursions to the countryside around the city that she undertook with one of our tenants. She planted them to replace the dead fruit trees. Firs, poplars and birches shot up and our part of the garden became a wooded grove. A horse-chestnut that my sister and I had planted under a hydrangea also grew into a mighty tree. The western side of the garden had, and still has, a very different aspect. Here the grass was cut regularly, colourful annuals filled the flower beds and white plastic chairs and tables completed the look of suburban propriety. The wild and neglected state of our part became one of the bones of contention in the long battle between the owner and my sister. Thirty years later, when she finally moved out, woodcutters had be called to fell our forest.

On the First Floor

THE FLATS ON THE FIRST and second floor, covering a surface of 200 square metres, were the largest and most luxuriously appointed in the building. As the ceiling of the first floor flat was 20 cm higher than that of the flat above, it had the higher volume of space, a circumstance I only noticed when looking at the section drawing of the design. On the other hand, the cantilevered balcony on the western side also distinguished the first floor flat and this could be seen at once from the outside. The client, Ferdinand Körösi, reserved this flat for his own use. It comprised the entire width and breadth of the building's surface with the exception of the communal stairwell. Three rooms connected by double doors and ornamented by stuccoed ceilings took up the side facing the street, while the narrow side was taken up by a bathroom and a chamber at one end and a further room with an adjacent veranda on the other. The kitchen, pantry, toilet and another room faced the garden. All the rooms were entered via the hallway. It was an arrangement not untypical for the bourgeois apartments of that era and neighbourhood.

Given that the economic situation in post-war Austria was only gradually getting better and that there was a lack of lodgers, especially since the owners were often unwilling to modernize the plumbing and the heating, quite a few of these flats remained empty or insufficiently maintained by the numerous widows with tenancies. It was almost impossible to find young girls from the country willing to light the fires in the tiled stoves, to drag the coal several flights of stairs from the cellar, or to polish the expanses of parquet flooring in exchange for food, lodgings and some pocket money. It was therefore not surprising that my mother, following the sudden death of our father, was able to find such a large flat at a price she could afford. She was not willing to stay in the country where our father had established a GP practice, and thus she had decided to return to her hometown. It so happened that friends knew of a flat that was about to become vacant in Geidorf, as the previous tenants wanted to move to the suburbs. My mother viewed the flat and on the spot decided to take it. We children had never seen such a suite of rooms before. We found the dark furniture, which the previous inhabitants took their own time to remove, heavy and oppressive; the leaded windows clinked at the slightest step as if they wanted to jump out of their frail frames; the high stuccoed ceilings weighed down on us. These impressions made the flat into a joyless place, appropriate to our new state as semi-orphans. It differed simply by its size from the home we had left behind forever, in the old building on the village's main square. There, we had lived in cramped conditions because our father's surgery had taken up most of the available space. This oppressive feeling in Number 31 slowly but surely abated, partly as we became accustomed to it and partly because of our mother's efforts to distribute the things we had brought with us in such a way that they seemed to have always been there. Even so, this first floor flat in Franckstrasse never became a home for me, but remained a temporary dwelling. The fact of my father's irrevocable absence was too clearly manifest – he had, after all, never set foot there, had never been present in any of the rooms; his feet had never hurried across the hallway, he had never shaved in the bathroom where the smell of his after-shave had never ever lingered, and he had never bent over the balcony railing to call to us in from the garden. Only in his sister's flat, in the nearby Bergmanngasse, had we ever all been together; I could imagine him there, but never in Franckstrasse 31.

My mother had a name plate mounted on the entrance door. It simply said LEICK. Even so, word got around that she was the widow of a physician and so, according to Austrian habit, the inhabitants of the house always addressed her as 'Frau Doktor'.

The Hallway

IN THE SOCIALLY determined spatial system of a city each neighbourhood or borough offers clues to the social level of the residents. In a city like Graz, divided by a river, the part that had been settled earliest usually has a higher social standing than the one incorporated at a later date. The inhabitants of the left bank regarded the right side of the river Mur, which became part of the city only in the 17th century, as poorer and less respectable. However, in any neighbourhood, it is the outer appearance of a building that forms the first impression, more or less imposing or modest, more or less dilapidated, newly built or ancient. Entering a building, it was the stairwell that set the tone, with or without stone steps, with or without a lift, well or badly plastered, with or without prevailing odours. In my time the doors of the old houses in the inner city were always unlocked during the day, and sometimes even at night, which meant that one could easily enter, have a look or sniff around, but it needed a reason or pretext to get inside the flats. The main door, once opened, gave onto the hallway not onto the dwelling space.

In the bourgeois houses of the early twentieth century, the hallway was a semi-private intermediary zone, where the visitor remained and waited to be told whether the master or mistress of the residence was willing or not to receive. The visitor might prefer to simply leave his or her card. While the masters moved from room to room through inter-connecting doors, staff had to enter these rooms through the hallway. In this way the intimate sphere of the residents was separated from the hallway that functioned as a serving space for the servants. Since this hallway did not benefit from direct ventilation, all sorts of odours accumulated, depending on the time of day and the time of the year. It could be any combination of the smell of cooking, of cleaning or polishing, of personal hygiene, smoking habits or floral arrangements, and there was a typical odour for each particular household that was immediately recognizable as such: here a smell of dog, there of cucumber salad or stewed apples, or cigarettes.

The hallway protected the private sphere of the residents which remained behind closed doors. Here one divested oneself of overclothes. This called for spacious wardrobes to accommodate coats and capes, umbrellas, walking sticks and head coverings. It needed a mirror and a console with a bowl to receive visiting cards, perhaps also a chair or two. The hallway could give a foretaste of the style in which the reception rooms would be furnished.

My favourite hallway in Graz was in the flat of my

godmother – the widow of a cultivated and eccentric lawyer – in Beethovenstrasse, because here one was greeted by an upright stuffed brown bear with wide open mouth showing his white fangs. His wild expression was terrible but even more terrible was the fact that he had to carry a silver platter in his black paws for the visiting cards. The walls were hung with ancient weaponry and darkened oil paintings and a dark red velvet curtain hung before the door to the salon. After such a theatrical entrance the salon itself was a disappointment; an anti-climax, despite the splendid old rugs and the choice furniture.

Our hallways in Franckstrasse 31 had no remarkable furnishings. It was immediately obvious that here rooms were let and that there were no masters. The factory-made runner had been chosen to be hard-wearing. There was no tray for visiting cards as those days were gone. My mother did not receive. She only had visitors from time to time, in contrast to her mother-in-law, who had maintained a grand house in Herdergasse and entertained a select company for tea, for bridge, and for dinners.

We no longer had a housemaid as my mother managed the household on her own. Except for the living-room, all the other rooms were used as bedrooms, not just for the family but also for the lodgers, and so the hallway resembled a guesthouse, where one met strangers in dressing-gowns hurrying to the bathroom, avoiding eye contact.

The etched glazing of the entrance door did not admit much light from the stairwell, and the dark brown gloss on doors and door frames rendered the space even darker, so that the hallway was always gloomy. Wooden wardrobes were used to store clothes unsuitable for the current season while a chest of drawers with a mirror above stood between the doorways. A framed etching showed a view of the Charles Bridge in Prague. My mother had bought this print in that city where she attended nursing college during the first years of the war. That this meant something in particular to her was not apparent from the etching. Between the kitchen door and the door to the toilet was a framed photograph, taken by a professional beach photographer: it showed us three children happily squinting from an inflatable raft in the Adriatic, during the last summer we had with our father.

There was a rail with hooks for coats in the eastern corner, and a shelf above for hats. Opposite stood a white Art Nouveau cupboard from the villa in Herdergasse which contained medicines and bandages from my father's day. Opening the door of this cupboard released a familiar smell of pharmaceuticals, redolent of his surgery. My mother took from it a packet of sanitary towels when I awoke one morning distraught, my pyjamas full of blood. She handed them over, saying that I should expect this to happen every month from now on and that it was normal for females.

On the western side was a large shipping trunk that had once belonged to my American grandmother, bearing her initials, MSH. The most precious thing in this shipping trunk was an old Slovenian folk costume from my mother's father's family, who came from Velika Nedelja, near Ptuj. This costume consisted of a white, handwoven linen skirt, heavily embroidered all over, a similarly embroidered blouse of the same material with wide sleeves, and a threadbare light-blue apron. A sudden whim prompted my mother to attack this trunk and the old Biedermeier mirror above it with oil paints in order to embellish it with folksy patterns.

The most important object in the hallway was the telephone that stood on a little table between my mother's room and the bathroom. Its cable was just about long enough for her to take the telephone to her room, but most of the calls had to made in the semi-public space of the hallway. Being on the telephone there, with lodgers in the offing, amounted to a per-formed intimacy – especially during prolonged calls: relationships inferred by silences, sighs, whispered sen-tences, murmured words or joyful cries, which might be overheard by whoever happened to be present in the hallway at the time.

The fact that the main door to the building was unlocked during the day allowed various mendicants, Mormons, Jehovah's Witnesses, travelling salesmen and pedlars to ring our doorbell. Such people had to be dealt with in the stairway, they were not admitted into the hallway. We were allowed to hand a piece of rye bread with lard to a beggar but not to let them eat in the kitchen, otherwise they would surely have come again. Tenants made their more or less vociferous complaints about us children through the barely-opened door. On the other hand, policemen wishing to talk to my mother about some misdemeanour committed by myself or my brother were freely admitted to the hallway, where they stood twirling their caps and looking around. That's how the Gestapo also used to stand in many a hallway in Austria during the war, asking questions or proceeding straightaway to an arrest, as our father's sister related. She had less reason to fear such a visit than many other people in Graz, a city that prided itself on the fact of having been the first Austrian city to attain the status of being *judenfrei*, rid of Jews. When the Russians arrived in Graz in 1945, whose violence against citizens was talked about much more than that of the Gestapo, the iron front door had been locked during the day. The Russians, so said Frau Azolla, had not been able to overcome the resistance of that splendid example of blacksmithing, and thus there had been no rape or other atrocity committed in this house.

The Living-Room

THE LIVING-ROOM, at the centre of three intercon-
nected rooms overlooking the street, was the most
sumptuous room in the apartment and the only one
with a large bay window ornamented with leaded,
coloured-glass panels. This did much to emphasize the
Old German, Master of Nuremberg atmosphere of the
living-room, which was also conveyed by the dark
green, highly ornamented ceramic stove. Only the Art
Nouveau decoration on the stuccoed ceiling was a con-
cession to comparatively modern times. All in all it was
an exemplary reception room for an apartment belonging to the German Nationalist high bourgeoisie of Graz.

My mother had furnished it with items from the
villa where my father had been raised; mahogany bookcases surmounted by old Chinese vases and silver can-
delabra, a highly wrought-iron, genuine Renaissance
chest, a well-stuffed armchair, the Bostonian great-
grandfather's portrait painted in oil, as well as the
framed photograph of his daughter in advanced years.
All these objects referred to our American rather than
our Austrian ancestors who had not managed to gener-
ate wealth or glory. A rose-wood chest of drawers and
framed prints of the emperor Napoleon and his wife

Josephine also came from my paternal grandmother's villa, remnants of its early nineteenth-century furnishings, when Louis Bonaparte had lived there in exile.

A finely woven silk carpet hung on the wall above a low sofa, while a highly floral Shiraz covered the parquet; both had been bought by my father who loved to surround himself with fine carpets. In the small flat we had inhabited in the country, most of the walls, beds and floors were covered with Oriental rugs and so it had always seemed to me the most perfectly cosy nest.

In this solidly middle-class living-room one would have expected at least a baby grand piano in the bay, where a string quartet would have been accommodated with ease, but instead the stage-like space, flanked by red velvet curtains, was devoted to a veneered cupboard that contained a radio at the bottom, a television in the middle and a record player at the top of it. The living-room's pride of place was therefore given to an example of the latest technology, which my father, who considered himself a modern man, had purchased in 1955, long before anyone else in the village. Turning the knobs of the radio receiver and waiting for a green eye to appear, one could eventually listen to the local radio stations and occasionally hear snatches of foreign stations, crystal clear for a few moments before they became a mere whirring noise. My father had bought some LPs for the record player, *Lucia di Lammermoor*,

Otello, *La forza del destino*, Max Bruch's First Violin Concerto, the *Per Gynt Suite*. My mother preferred popular music singles by Connie Francis or Freddy Quinn. My aunt sent us the first Beatles LPs – that I played again and again for hours at a time, interspersed with my *Anitra's Dance*. Lying on the Persian carpet in the middle of the room, I tried to let the classical music takes its effect, to understand it. However, we weren't a musical family and we didn't subscribe to concerts of classical music. My mother said that she had been forced to take piano lessons, which she hated.

None of us children showed musical talent or an inclination to learn to play a musical instrument. At school we had to choose between Drawing and Music, an irreversible choice once taken. Our art teacher, himself an artist, took us to see exhibitions of modern art and he made us feel the singular pleasure that the contemplation of a painting or a piece of sculpture could produce. The lack of musical education made it hard to appreciate music that aimed at more than entertainment. Listening again and again to the Bruch Violin Concerto or the *Per Gynt Suite* was an attempt to enter into the music, much as how, with some books, one has to make an effort to get into the text, but the sounds were simultaneous, intertwined and overlaid, and I quickly lost my bearings. I would not even start on the operas because I could not cope with the violent emotions, especially intense when conveyed by Maria

Callas, and also because it reminded me too painfully of the times when my father had played these records, far too loudly for our small residence in the village.

Listening to the radio or to records was a solitary undertaking, when I managed to excuse myself from a family outing. Watching television, however, was something that bound the family together. While the radio offered a choice between regional and national stations, back then there was only one television station, based in Vienna. At the beginning of the programme a voice always intoned the various federal transmitters placed on mountains near the respective federal capitals; the solemn recitation of their names – *Jauerling, Kahlenberg, Semmering, Patscherkofel, Pyramidenkogel, Sonnwendstein,* etc, invoked the unification of the nation into a television community, into a television family.

In the evening, once the dishes for supper had been cleared away, we assembled in the living-room in front of the television, my mother in one of the armchairs that was moved to the centre of the room and us children on various Turkish or Moroccan pouffes. Austrian television in the early 1960s was closely associated with the theatre and cabarets and relied on actors who appeared on stage. We all liked some of the early series: black and white soap operas that showed life in middle-class Viennese families, while we were less taken by those talk shows that patronized either children or older people. There were also special occasions, much trumpeted, when Germanophone Swiss, German and Austrian national stations united to present lavish quiz shows with musical interludes to a supra-national community of viewers.

My favourite televised events were the skiing races. I had a crush on an ace downhill skier from Vorarlberg, who triumphed over his competitors on the iciest runs and foggiest courses down the steepest slopes.

This communal viewing of television united the family. We sat quietly together, all eyes on the set, only rarely making a comment, until at nine o'clock my mother turned off the set and we all went to bed. It was a sign of being almost grown-up to be allowed to stay until the end of transmission at eleven o'clock when the national anthem was played over images of our red and white flag billowing in the wind. By the time my sister and I were old enough to be allowed to stay up that late we had lost all interest. We preferred to meet our friends outside. For a while my mother sat with my younger brother and then eventually alone before the television set.

Visitors, mainly women who wanted to confide in my mother, were shown into the living-room, where she served them sandwiches and coffee while they talked about their unhappy marriages. My mother was known to be a good listener. She did not particularly appreciate these visits and did little to encourage them. More intimate friends were shown into the kitchen. She did not receive guests, we had no dinner parties or evening invitations. My mother was too proud to be a hostess without a man at her side and given the absence of domestic help she did not want the bother of having to serve her guests and carry everything in from the kitchen.

The living-room served as a showcase for the beautiful apartment and as a place for familial rituals, which consisted essentially of the nightly TV viewing, apart from the Christmas celebration. For this event members of my father's fraternity would deliver a large spruce that had served for their Yule Feast that was celebrated before the Christian one. This tree reached right up to the 4.30 m-high ceiling and the extra-long ladder had to be fetched from the cellar. My mother spent hours decorating the tree, fastening hundreds of small chocolates wrapped in printed aluminium foil, colourful glass baubles and bells, as well as little wax candles in special holders onto the branches of the tree.

On Christmas Eve after lunch, we took the bus to the cemetery at the outskirts of the city. There were miniature Christmas trees set up on the snow-covered graves, with tiny candles like those on birthday cakes flickering in the darkening afternoon. On the way home we could see the candles people had placed by their windows in remembrance of the Fallen and here

54

and there we had a glimpse of Christmas trees where the candles had already been lit.

Finally we stood before our own Christmas wonder. The ignited sparklers spread their exciting gunpowder smell, the wax dripped onto the dark green branches and we listened to the recording of *Silent Night* sung by the Vienna Boys' Choir. We stood there and looked at the beautiful tree and avoided looking at our mother, who was always very sad on this occasion. A chance remark by her own mother or by her sister-in-law, who had both been invited for the occasion, would be enough to hurt her feelings and to produce a most uncomfortable atmosphere. In later years we children fled as soon as possible, once the presents had been opened.

My mother would remain with her mother, with whom she did not get on well, and look at the Christmas tree where the candles had burnt out, surrounded by the Christmassy smell of wax and spruce also associated with the cemetery.

The Bedroom

THE BEDROOM, as we called my mother's room, was located on the western side, between the living-room and the bathroom and opposite the kitchen. When we moved into the flat in the autumn of 1960, all three of us children slept there with our mother. We had been used to being packed together, as in the country the whole family slept in one attic room, the parents behind a thin curtain. As cosy as this attic had appeared, with its low and crooked walls and two small windows, so strange and unfriendly did that large bedroom appear to us; and we huddled around our mother in the double bed as chicks around a hen. She nailed an oriental carpet to the wall behind her bed, a Senneh. We could stroke the soft pile when we woke at night, anxious at the sound of unfamiliar creaking in the parquet floor, steps from the flat above or other noises from the street.

The previous tenant, who moved to a modern house in the suburbs, left various items of furniture behind – Biedermeier wardrobes, chests of drawers, curtains and curtain rails, as well as an oil painting. This picture, a full size 19th century copy of Lucas Cranach's *Madonna of Innsbruck*, hung between the two windows, exactly opposite my mother's bed. When she sat up, she looked straight at the Madonna, who in turn looked at the viewer in an encouraging, if also a sad way. Her son, a sturdy peasant boy, does not, as in so many other pictures of this kind, look out of the picture in a prematurely wise or forgiving manner. Instead he is turned towards his mother, reaching for her cheek, desiring that all her attention be focused on him, and this seems to please the young woman, even though she does not return his gaze but looks out of the picture.

In contrast to her own mother, our mother was not a believer. She never went to mass, thought little of the Catholic church and spoke contemptuously of the clergy. This painting, the only one in the flat to have any connection to Christian religion, was not a sacred image for her. As long as she lived, it stayed on the wall opposite the matrimonial bed, which she was never to share with a man again.

She also hung another painting in her bedroom, her own portrait, which was done in March 1939, according to a notice on the stretcher. A painter in Graz, Rolf Ubell – I don't know how he had made her acquaintance – had asked the then 15-year-old Herta Schescherko to sit for him. He had received a commission for a large painting that was to show *The German Youth in Contemplation of the German Flag at Candle Light*. In preparation he painted some studies in oil, not just of Herta Schescherko, but also of a blond youth, who was sometimes present in the studio and with whom she was a little in love. She said that he fell in the war, quite early on. It seems that the large painting was only a pretext, since Rolf Ubell did not belong to those artists in Graz who used their talent for the glorification of the National Socialists. In the picture, the girl hardly looks like a typical Aryan maiden, with her dark hair, her eyebrows nearly joined in the middle, her eyes dark in the candle light. She looks expectantly, with interest, at the artist.

With the exception of this portrait, nothing in that room remained from the time before my mother's marriage. She rarely talked about her parental home in the Naglergasse. After the early death of her father, who had been more than twenty years older than her mother and who she had loved very much, and after her mother had married her husband's best friend, which she did within a year, she did not have a pleasant time there. She was happy to join the proto-Nazi Youth Groups, which offered a chance to escape the stifling, Catholic, lower middle-class atmosphere of her home.

There was also nothing in this room that evidenced it as the room of a woman. There was no dressing table and no visible cosmetics, no potted plants, no knick-knacks. It was a serious, sombre room; the Baroque writing desk from Herdergasse in one corner and the two Biedermeier wardrobes on either side of the closed door to the living-room. Nothing was ever left lying about here. Everything was tidy, all clothes stored in the wardrobes. There were no piles of paper on the desk, no empty glass by the bed. The wooden shutters were usually closed to prevent the carpets from fading.

The dominant colour in this room was a reddish brown, caused in the first instance by the Senneh rug above the bed, with its umbra containing tiny flecks of orange. Further contributing to this Rembrandt mood, deep red prevailed in both paintings – in the darkened copy of the Cranach and also in the portrait of my mother in candle light, where she wears a rust-red blouse with red-golden stripes. It was in this room, in the matrimonial bed beneath the russet Senneh, that in 1976 our mother suffered a haemorrhage, from the consequences of which she died a few days later.

The Master's Room

THE EASTERNMOST of the three representative rooms linked by double doors could have been the master's room (*Herrenzimmer*), reserved for the use of the husband. I don't know if Mr Körösi had been married when he lived in the flat, but it seemed rather too large for a bachelor living alone. My grandfather had identified his room in my grandmother's villa in the Herdergasse as such, writing *Herrenzimmer* below the photographs taken by a professional photographer in an album that documented the furnishings of the villa. One could see here a low sofa, covered with furs and Caucasian carpets, some occasional tables for ashtrays and drinks, a man's desk, where he dealt with his correspondence, and on the wall pictures of his ancestors, together with a portrait of his wife.

Since we had no father in our household – no master – this room did not become a master's room but a children's room, as soon as we were ready to leave mother's bed. On the rough weave of a Persian nomad carpet our brother played with his cars, and there we could romp and fight each other when we felt like it, or look at picture books, lying flat on our stomachs.

I remember a large picture that our mother had hung there, a black framed print of the famous painting *George Washington Crossing the Delaware*. Our American grandmother had brought it with her as a reminder of her Republican origins, and she displayed it in the various apartments and houses she shared with her Austrian officer husbands during the monarchy and thereafter. Had she still been alive, she would have been able to tell us the story of the crossing. We saw a boat full of soldiers on the turbulent waters of the river, some rowing, some gesticulating, looking anxiously at the shore, while the general with his tricorn hat, wrapped in a coat flapping in the storm, stood upright with an expression of unwavering determination while behind him the flag-bearer grasped the tightly rolled star-spangled banner that surmounted the scene. This picture had already faded and it was too high on the wall to be able to examine it properly. After a while our mother had it taken down to be stored in the cellar compartment, to where she had also relegated other objects from the Herdergasse villa, even some valuable ones.

Her relationship with her mother-in-law had been tense. This woman, described by all who had known her as a forceful personality, came from a wealthy Bostonian background. With her doctorate from Johns Hopkins University and her tenderness for my father, she had been an almost invincible rival in the fight for the husband's love. This fight had begun when in 1950 my father had invited his mother to live in the house he rented on a Carinthian lake, where he had opened his first practice. After a year of passive resistance – I was born at the beginning of 1951 – the grandmother returned to Graz. My father made a second attempt in the mid-fifties to have his mother, whom he loved and admired, come to live with his family. The unflagging resistance of his wife however, as well as the spatial constraints of the small flat in the village, where his practice had better success than in Carinthia, had forced the mother-in-law to retreat. She then went to live with her younger daughter in London where she died soon after. It is therefore not surprising that my mother could only tolerate those objects originally belonging to her mother-in-law that had already been in the flat in the country and hence part of our life. There had been no room there for that Washington picture.

The three of us children spent about a year or a bit longer in the children's room, then one of the lodgers moved out and I was given his room. Soon afterwards my sister was also granted a room of her own, next to the kitchen. Our brother remained alone in the large children's room, despite the fact that he was the youngest of the siblings. I do not recall that this ever gave rise to quarrels. My brother stayed there until he left the flat in his mid-twenties. He was four years younger than me and three years younger than my sister. His birth had given rise to celebrations in the family – at last a boy! We had not been very taken with this lemon-headed, red-faced infant, but eventually he turned into a hardy brother who let us have our rough and tumble ways with him. He was only five years old when our father had had his accident and he hardly remembered our life in the country. He had something wrong with his eyes and had to wear thick-lensed glasses, one eye taped up to correct a cast. He could hold his own on the way to school; for him the Franckstrasse was a battle-ground where fierce fights and ambushes had to be braved. He often came home bruised and with his glasses broken. He was not one for learning and paying attention at school and his far-sightedness made reading troublesome. As teenagers my sister and I hardly found his company stimulating, while he pre-ferred to spend his time with his friends. He was loving towards our mother, although he had little time for her. He was very attractive to women. He took after our father in this respect, who was at times hard pressed to ward off the attentions of women who fancied him.

During the time when my sister and I studied abroad, my brother lived alone with my mother. The lodgers had all left long ago and my mother had begun to work in the maternity department of the hospital as a social worker in charge of adoptions. My brother was mainly out, with friends, or with girlfriends, and would just appear at meal times. He would also stay away for days. However, our mother was glad not be utterly alone in this large flat. It was he who rang for the ambulance when she collapsed at his door. He was the only one of us able to see her before she died in hospital a few days later.

Except for the pretty, white ceramic stove with a frieze of dancing nymphs surrounding a long-haired, wet-looking Neptune, there was nothing remarkable to see in this room. But if I can only dimly remember its furnishings, several episodes stayed in my mind that had to do with sexuality, however unclear this connection had been at the time. Still, the various emotions – the curiosity, the excitement, and also the shame and disgust, made a deep impression.

Despite being the offspring of a doctor and living in the countryside, we indulged in fantastic notions when it came to procreation. We had heard all sorts of rumours, promulgated by the blacksmith' daughter: that babies got into their mother's body through the navel and that they were born from the anus, that older boys liked to suck milk from their girlfriends' breasts but that the touching of some parts of the body was unchaste. My mother tried several times to talk about such things in a reasonable manner but I always found the topic embarrassing. Back then, I did not want to know and insisted on my ignorance.

One evening, when our mother had left us in the care of one of the lodgers, at a time when the three of us still slept in the children's room, we got into a state of excitement, stimulated by the fact that the lodger, who occupied the adjoining room, was alone with his fiancée, who had been allowed to stay. We wanted to hear what was going on next door and crept to the locked double door that separated the two rooms. We must have giggled too much, at any rate the lodger stormed in and sternly bade us go back to bed. We worried that he might tell our mother, but he didn't.

The second incident engraved on my mind occurred during a visit by my father's sister, our much-loved aunt from London. For some reason she did not stay at her sister's flat in the Bergmanngasse that night and my mother had let her have the use of the children's room, while my brother slept in her bedroom. In the morning I wanted to see if our aunt was up and when I opened the door I was stunned to see the hairy, naked bottom of a man protruding from the bedcovers and I saw the aunt lying there too in that narrow child's bed. I was so shocked that I ran straight my mother to tell her that I had seen a man with a bare bottom. The incident led to embarrassing scenes, for our aunt held me responsible. How could anyone simply open the door to a room where grown-ups were sleeping? The man in the bed was identified as Uncle Heini, a friend of my aunt's whom we knew quite well from previous visits. It was the last time that this aunt stayed the night in our flat.

My mother forbade the lodgers to receive female company and when one night she came across a rather louche woman, who calmly blew the smoke of her cigarette in her face when challenged before disappearing into a lodger's room, that lodger was gone the next day. My father's sisters, our aunts – so our maternal grandmother liked to tell us – had not enjoyed a good reputation and were well known all over Graz for their many love affairs. Our mother feared that we might have a similar disposition, but all her efforts at preventing this remained fruitless and we, rather proudly, continued the tradition.

My brother could not be stopped from receiving his girlfriends. He simply locked the door when he wanted some privacy, after our mother had surprised him once in the act.

Years later, when I no longer lived in Franckstrasse 31 but still had a key to the flat, I arrived with two friends while no one was at home. Thus it happened that the transition from a conventional relationship between two people to a less conventional between three people took place in the master's room, on the double bed that had by then become my brother's.

The Parlour Maid's Room

THE ARCHITECT Louis Kahn developed a theory that differentiated served spaces from serving spaces. The former are actively used rooms, while the latter facilitate the proper functioning of these primary rooms. He understood serving spaces to be those used for ventilation, for heating, for the connection between floors. However, the same distinction had been made long before, in communally occupied dwellings where the living quarters of certain persons, be it out of respect for their advanced age as in China or because of their higher social standing, were more comfortably appointed and better furnished than those of socially inferior persons in same household. In the large apartments in Franckstrasse the rooms giving onto the street were reserved for the masters, while those overlooking the garden were servant spaces, given over as work places and sleeping quarters for the domestic staff.

To the left of the entrance door was a narrow room, corresponding in size to the water closet and the adjoining pantry on the other side of the entrance. It was originally divided into two – one space to store visitors' overcoats, hats, umbrellas and canes, and another behind a partition that served as bedroom for the house-

maid. In the year we moved into the flat, a lodger occupied this room. When my mother decided to give
each of the children a room to themselves my brother
was given the master's room, while my sister and I had
to make do with former servant's rooms – with which
we were perfectly happy.

They were our virginal chambers, incubation spaces
for growing up, where we spent the last years of childhood and the first years of puberty. My mother bought
a bed with a headboard for my room, plus a wall-
mounted bookcase with two drawers, and she let me
have the round table from our previous flat and two
low, upholstered chairs. I had my own wardrobe and
there was a Bosnian kilim on the floor by the bed.

My favourite spot was the window-sill, built into
the thickness of the outer wall. In this window-niche I
sat with my legs drawn up, leaning against the wall,
pressed into an intermediate space between inside and
outside. On summer nights I could look down at the
gardens below me and at the moon moving behind
ever changing configurations of clouds. In the winter,
there was a bolster between the inner and outer window to keep out the cold, which made it possible to use
the window-sill even during the cold.

In this chamber I began to read, an activity which
was to determine my whole life. It became imperative
to have enough reading material and I was always
anxious about running short. The two glazed bookcases

in the living-room were kept locked. They had belonged to the paternal grandmother and still contained the many leather-bound editions of American and English classics, as well as her medical textbooks. All these books were in the original language and hence inaccessible to me. There were some books in German that had belonged to my father. My mother let me borrow one or another of these books; I could have Turgenev, the historical novels of Stefan Zweig, as well as the German and Greek heroic tales or *The Three Musketeers*, which my father had read as a boy. Books that might be kept were only given us on special occasions, and we had to save up our pocket money for quite a while before we could buy a paperback. I don't remember who had given me the three volumes of the *Die Höhlenkinder im heimlichen Grund* (The Cave Children of the Secret Glade). I was so enchanted with this that I henceforth only wanted historical books for Christmas. Each year I discovered another volume to my great delight: *Prehistory, The History of the Ancient Near East, The History of Egypt, The History of Classical Antiquity*. I loved the names of the countries and the cities, of the kings and of the gods: Sumer, Uruk, Nineveh, Hammurabi, Ashurbanipal, Tuthmosis, Hatshepsut, Alcibiades, Theoderic. I liked to look at the chronological charts of successive dynasties, intermediate periods and migrations, and I enjoyed the maps and the illustrations of archaeological ruins. The reading of these books needed concentration and patience, and the window niche was good for that. Reading the history books was a slow process, with intervals to digest the information, and this differed from the reading of books devoured at night in bed. My habit of reserving the reading of fiction for the evening goes back to this time. We were given books deemed suitable for growing girls, most often written in the time between the wars and these had been read by our mother at the same age – books in which lively, somewhat tomboyish virgins eventually submitted with good humour to their allotted fate as wives and mothers. Such books were very easy to read, they had been written to convey to adolescent girls that true happiness was to be found in having a family life. The greedy, rapid way of tearing through such books was also suitable for the adventure stories that I continued to read with the aid of a torch after my mother had turned off the light. One had to read fast to find out if and how the heroes had managed to escape from some peril. Here one could submit to the feelings that the narrator intended to arouse, rejoicing over an escape at the last minute, admiring the noble spirit of the courageous hero, crying bitterly at the end, when it was a bitter end. The novels of Karl May were the first adventure books to delight me. They became an addiction and it was insufferable not to have the next volume at hand. The spontaneous offer by a girl at school, whom I had ignored until then, to let me read the third volume of the *Winnetou* trilogy, marked the beginning of a lifelong friendship. The enthusiasm for Karl May was encouraged by adult males of my mother's acquaintance, who had read the same stories with the same fervour in their own youth. However, the time came when it became impossible for me to read another line of Karl May. Instead I discovered the adventure books in the paternal store: *The Three Musketeers*, *The Last of the Mohicans*, *Treasure Island*, *The Red Corsair*.

To balance the time spent reading there was sport. I enrolled in various youth clubs and trained in several disciplines – athletics, swimming and gymnastics. The word *Leibesübung* (bodily exercises) described these activities well enough. A musical child always practises the same movements of fingers, arms and airways to acquire the facility to master an instrument so that it becomes part of the body. The athletic child also tries to achieve mastery through repetition. I was interested in learning the right technique to perform the front crawl, the 100 metre sprint, the high jump, etc. I wanted to have a quickly reacting, toughened body and I was proud of my hard muscles and my broad shoulders. My room was permeated with the smell of embrocation to treat sore muscles and tendons. Physical Exercise was the only subject listed in the school reports where I always had the best marks.

My worst subject was mathematics and my mother had to pay students to give me private tuition at home. We sat at my round table on the low upholstered chairs, bent over the notebooks in a forced intimacy that interfered with my concentration on equations. None of these tutors managed to improve my inability to deal with numbers; at best they helped me get a pass grade or prevent – and that not always – an oral examination at the beginning of the school year.

It was the first time that I had a room of my own. One was left alone, sometimes even sent there in punishment, from the kitchen or the living-room. We children rarely visited each other and then mainly with the intention to disrupt. But it was always possible to simply lock the door. My mother only entered to wake us up in the morning, to say Good Night, or to do a bit of dusting during the day. We made the beds ourselves and tidied our clothes away.

The parlour maid's room was a place of becoming, of transformation from child to nubile girl. Rumours sprung up at school whenever one of the pupils would not participate in physical exercises. We would put an arm around the girl's shoulders to find out if she were already wearing a brassière. I had no idea what was going on and I hardly knew more when I began to have periods quite a bit later than the others in my class because of all the training I did. Just as mysterious was a burning interest that could suddenly be set alight by a photograph, a very fleeting encounter on the street, a scene in a movie. Longer-lasting crushes could amount to a sort of adoration; many in my class thus worshipped our sporty and impeccably impartial Latin teacher. I adored one of the Austrian ski stars, Karl Schranz from Sankt Anton, world champion in the downhill and overall winner of the world championship in Chamonix 1962, silver medallist in giant slalom at the Olympic Games in Innsbruck; he had invented his own style, tucking the sticks under his armpits while he plummeted down the steep runs in a low squat. I wrote to him ardent letters of congratulation, keen to express my everlasting admiration. He sent me postcards with his photograph, signed by himself, and I looked at this face with the strong dark eyebrows and the dazzling white teeth with rapture. It was part of one's publicly-avowed adoration to be teased for it; in fact, accepting such derision with equanimity was a tribute to the object of veneration. I also adored a French actor, but only in his guise as Winnetou, chief of the Apaches, in the film version of the Karl May novels. I stuck images of my two crushes, cut from magazines, on my headboard, and kissed them good night before going to sleep.

One could also have a crush on a fellow pupil or a teacher. My best friend had a face I loved to look at and we walked about the school corridors with our arms around each other. All these crushes and friendships, which differed from the comradeship of childhood by increased tenderness, were stages in the learning curve about love. A certain face could cause feelings that differed from all feelings previously felt, an attraction that could be pondered without being able to understand it any better.

Certainly I knew more about death than I did about love. When a retired plasterer suffered a fatal heart attack in my room, it was an unforgettable but not a shocking sight. A burst pipe, caused by the refusal of the tenants above to heat this part of the flat during the winter, had been repaired and the hole needed to be plastered over. My mother found a pensioner prepared to do the job for cash in hand. He pushed the bed aside and climbed the long ladder he'd had to fetch from the cellar, holding on to a bucket of mortar and his trowel. I was in the hallway when I heard a loud noise and on opening the door I saw the man lying on the floor, his face dark blue. He was, as my mother immediately saw, without breath or heartbeat. The deceased labourer, so we heard from the widow afterwards, had been repeatedly warned by his doctor not to get up tall ladders because of his high blood pressure. The hole above my bed remained unfilled for quite a while and reminded me of the workman who died doing his job. His was not the first corpse I had seen. We had watched several dead people lying in state in their coffins and had not been afraid of them. We had also been exposed to the sight of heavily wounded or lifeless bodies in car wrecks or lying mangled on the road, because our father, being a doctor, had a duty to stop at the site of an accident and to render what aid he could until the arrival of an ambulance. We children watched the proceedings from the back of the car in which my father himself was to become the victim of a crash.

Not long after my first period, my mother decided that I should move into the previous lodger's room with the adjoining veranda, because that last remaining lodger preferred to rent the cheaper maid's room which had already ceased to be a maid's room.

The Veranda

ON THE NORTH-EASTERN side of the two major flats a special room concluded the *enfilade* of spaces to emphasize the view over the garden. According to the initial plans it was originally designed as a semi-open terrace, but this was never realized, perhaps because the north-west orientation would never have provided enough sunlight or warmth. The compromise was a wintery space, referred to as the veranda – glazed on two sides, with the other walls clad in light pine panelling. It was a room that could only be used during the summer, as there was no heating and the single-glazed windows could not keep the cold at bay. In the summer though, one could feel here as if one were on holiday.

My mother furnished the veranda with the contents of my father's waiting-room – the solid wooden square table spread with a green velvet cloth and the corner bench that went with it. She also hung there the pictures that had been in the waiting-room: framed reproductions of Dürer's water-colours. The velvet cloth still smelled faintly of the old waiting-room, of stable and hayloft, fresh wood, home-grown tobacco, and of soap, as much as the flat did on Sundays.

By the time I was assigned the previous lodger's room this smell had all but disappeared. I could do what I liked on the veranda. I slept there, and there I entertained my friends. Because of its relative remoteness and because of the wide views through the glazed wall, the room suggested a feeling of spontaneity and freedom. It was a friendly summer room. Only the small spiders that proliferated here were disagreeable, and their bites left long itching welts. Disagreeable too were the gnats whose persistent humming disturbed one's sleep during the sultry nights.

The Lodger's Room

DURING THE 1930s, a modernist, three-storey apartment block was built on the empty lot on the eastern side of Franckstrasse 31. The new building reduced the daylight that could fall into the rooms opposite. In our flat only one room was affected, the one between the master's room next to the veranda. The single glazing of the veranda made it hard also to heat this room adequately and the heavy dark curtains that were meant to insulate it created an even gloomier atmosphere. However, during the summer, both rooms were agreeable enough.

When we first moved into the flat my mother let these rooms to students. This was meant to bolster her meagre widow's pension and to bridge the gap between the posting and the arrival of the monthly cheque from America. We children had been granted the right to enter into my father's share of the great-grandfatherly fortune and the interest accruing until the time of our respective majorities was made available to my mother in order to give us a proper education.

The lodgers she chose were medical students and they had to be members of the fraternity *Germania*. Since my father had joined this fraternity himself his widow had the right to claim affiliation to their social functions. Just after we had moved in, at the beginning of the autumn term, three students began to live with us: two brothers from Upper Austria and one from Lübeck in Germany, who was not willing to brave the winter in the veranda and so did not return after the Christmas break.

These lodgers, people who did not belong to the family, could not help but make their presence felt. Their footsteps, their repressed laughter and whispers, echoed in the hallway. They occupied the bathroom and the toilet where they left their smells. We found their student habits and mannerisms intriguing. It was one of the rules of this type of fraternity that new recruits had to show their manliness and their courage by fighting a duel using a sabre and without wearing a face shield. Snapshots showed them wearing thigh-high black boots, tight breeches, white shirts with billowing sleeves and wadded waistcoats, each wielding the naked blade. They also showed the result of these combats – faces streaming with blood. Stitched up straight away, the resulting scar was a permanent reminder of the combatant's courage and commitment.

The lodgers used their rooms primarily for sleeping. They took their meals at the students' canteen or in the fraternity's favoured guesthouse. They spent the days either in the lecture rooms or the fraternity's headquarters and their evenings in compatible drinking places. It was an important part of their student life to acquire the ability to hold large quantities of alcohol, primarily beer and *Schnaps*, as suitably Germanic beverages. The ability to handle drink also became part of our own education, once my sister and I were of an age to be taken to their festivities.

I rarely entered the lodgers' rooms, and then only when they were out of the house or when I helped my mother with the dusting. There were stacks of papers and text-books and I had to be careful not to throw out one of the prepared medical specimens, a finger or some cartilage. The older brother completed his studies first. He was a good-humoured young man and the scar across his nose gave him a dashing appearance. After he moved out his younger brother remained the sole occupant for some years. He took an interest in the history and the ideological foundations of the fraternity and endorsed its German-nationalist ideals. His nature was less sunny than that of his brother. He had a tendency to brood and his sarcasm could be biting and hurtful. He was my mother's ally in the fights I had with her once I was old enough to challenge her continuing enthusiasm for the *Führer*. When he moved out, having finished his degree, I was given this room. He remained close to my mother and this relationship helped her to bear her loneliness once my sister and I had left home.

The lodger's room was to have new furnishings – I was allowed to choose the fabrics for the curtains and the new upholstery. The connecting door between it and the master's room was permanently closed when a wardrobe was built into the recess. I carried on sleeping in my virgin's bed. In addition to my old round table, there was a large desk. I was meant to be a diligent student in this room as only a few more school years remained until the university entrance exams. I was barely interested in the curriculum and paid just about enough attention for a pass grade. In this always rather dark room I preferred to spend my time under the reading lamp devouring works of world literature. I read the great novels of the Russians, the Germans, the English, the French, gaining access to the world of great emotions and of love; to worlds, times and societies that were strange to me. I learnt to pay attention to the manner of writing – whether it used long or short sentences, resounding or quiet tones, or whether it was composed thoughtfully or impetuously. Thus I discovered in me a never to be stilled desire for literature. In those years I also developed two reading habits: firstly, to read every book I began to the last page, never to jump to another section or stop altogether, unless the book was particularly trivial – and secondly, to read the original rather than a translation, as far as possible, constantly referring to dictionaries and misunderstanding most of the text. Some works demanded repeated and careful reading – *The Man without Qualities*, *War and Peace*, *Elective Affinities* – while the works of other authors were exhausted after a single reading, those by Thomas Mann for instance, or Franz Werfel, or Hermann Hesse. It was also fortunate for me that there was an institution called *Forum Stadtpark* in Graz, where one could listen to authors reading from texts they had just written, and where the people who went to these readings would recommend other books and texts that they deemed essential to know. Gradually the range of available sources of reading grew from the bookcases at home to include the county library, the second-hand bookshops and the flea markets, as well as to newly published paperbacks for which one had to save up.

The time not spent in this room was spent on other aspects of growing up – on friendship and on love. My one or two close friends at school whispered the right answers during any oral exam, read the same books and had the same need to discuss everything that moved us in great detail. They kept secrets – nearly everything concerning our inner world was secret – and in turn confided their fears, hopes and excitements. Jointly suffered humiliations and punishments meted out by our teachers only strengthened these bonds, as did jointly experienced adventures, joys and triumphs. The pleasure we took in each other, the mutual tempting, was even more important. The confusing feelings and reactions we felt when being looked at by a male; the blushing, the anxiety, and at the same time the desire to look back at him, even if only surreptitiously, to see if he was looking, all this we experienced more or less at the same time, and we compared notes on whom we could possibly like or who would simply be impossible to imagine as a boyfriend. Having a boyfriend was something quite different from having a girlfriend.

A boyfriend was a step towards having a steady boyfriend, which in turn was a step towards a fiancé who in turn could become a husband, if this sequence ran its course without disruption. One of our classmates, who had until then been completely unremarkable, suddenly had to leave school because she got pregnant by her boyfriend who ended up marrying her. At that time, when we sometimes saw her pushing the pram, very few of the girls in my class had a boyfriend. Each was meant to keep their virginity at least until after the final exams had been successfully passed and their parents did their best to ensure that they remained intact. A boyfriend endangered the virginal status, because a boyfriend wanted more. He wanted more than to sit on some park bench holding hands or to snog a bit during a movie or to dance closely at the disco. The girlfriend at times also wanted more than that.

I was fully prepared to meet the advances of a good-looking Serbian lad during a holiday on a Croatian island in the summer of 1965, but my mother made sure that this did not go beyond the exchange of passionate kisses. Two years later, when I still had not managed to secure a boyfriend and was busy with all my athletic pursuits, a gynaecologist prescribed the then newly invented contraceptive pill to regularize my periods that the hard training made so irregular. In this way I was safe from the unwanted consequences of having a boyfriend even before I had one and therefore I set out to find an object of desire, a boyfriend, one who did not live in Belgrade but in Graz. It was fortuitous that my girlfriend's mother allowed us to make use of her deceased grandmother's empty flat, ostensibly for the purpose of doing homework. There was a cheap canteen on a floor above that flat, very popular with the students from the nearby technical university. It did not take long before my chosen candidate had become my lover. His to me irresistible smile, in a mouth filled with white but crooked teeth, his cord jeans and flower-patterned shirts, his longish hair and cool elegance made him, as far as I was concerned, the most desirable man in Graz. On top of that he had already completed his degree in architecture and worked as a lecturer in the department of interior design. He had his own little flat in the outskirts of Graz and drove an Austin Mini. I calmed his reservations about me being a minor and introduced him at home where his charm made the right impression. I cancelled my memberships at the sports clubs and began my sex life.

This took place in my lover's basement flat, not in Franckstrasse 31, where the time spent without him became torturous. I looked to literature for inspiring female characters, I admired the gentle decisiveness of Vrenchen, the wild abandon of Grushenka. How to bear the time until the next phone call? How to free oneself from schoolgirl passivity? I was lucky that my lover was patient and really rather fond of me, although I was not his official girlfriend. She was not a schoolgirl but a grown-up and a model and she worked in Rome. On the rare occasions she came to visit I made myself scarce. I was not even jealous of this woman I knew only from photographs – wearing heavy make-up, mini-skirts and white patent leather boots, because after all he spent most of his time with me. He took his first dose of LSD with me, took me to design fairs where we slept next to his mini near the motorway when none of our acquaintances could offer us a bed.

There was less and less time for homework. I fought, rarely successfully, against the impulse to take the train back to his flat in the suburbs and to wait there for him. My mother said that I should make myself less readily available; it makes a woman more desirable to a man than for her to throw herself at him. She also warned me not to squander myself on fruitless love affairs but to seek and find the right man. She had only found my father after several abortive attempts, and that she was not able to keep him was simply a matter of fate. The floundering of the love affairs and marriages of his two sisters on the other hand, were caused by egoism and jealousy, for which she blamed the aunts rather than their men. The right sort of man seemed to me an invention of a bygone era. I came to think it better to find a suitable man for a certain time of one's life; at least this insight was a fruit of the apprenticeship in love during the years spent in the veranda room.

All the reading, the friends, comrades and lovers could not quieten my inner restlessness. I wanted out, away from this flat, away from Graz, away from the circumscribed life of a school-girl. Again and again, I stood on one of the streets leading out of the city and accepted lifts from drivers who had stopped, private cars or lorries, willing to take me for a ride. It was very easy to hitch lifts. The drivers could not see from their vehicles whether a male or a female was standing there with outstretched thumb, because my hair was cut so short and I was usually wearing jeans and a bomber jacket or an anorak. I found enchantment in the most mundane places I happened to have arrived at by pure chance, places that were quite unremarkable, without a view or an architectural monument, where nothing special was going on or had ever been going on – just very ordinary street corners and motorway slip-roads. Simply being there at this moment in time, at this particular place, a place I would most likely never see again, was thrilling: it also gave me a great surge of freedom. This caused a little shiver, of the sort one experiences in front of a great work of art which one only dares to look at from the corner of an eye.

I had no desire for the East, not the Near East, the Middle East nor the Far East but was attracted by the West – by England and by Ireland. My sister wanted to go East, the farther the better and so she took the Paris–New Delhi Magic Bus to India. This was a much greater adventure than my aimless hitch-hiking. Emaciated, full of vermin and intestinal parasites, she was delivered back home by a Buddhist couple, originally from Denmark, who had taken care of her, made her sip warm tea, and had been looking after her night and day and so saved her life. My sister was so impressed with their selfless devotion that she decided to give up her art history course in Paris in order to take up the study of Sanskrit and Tibetan and eventually became a Buddhist herself. When she then took over the veranda room for a while it became like the cell of a Tibetan nun, filled with scroll paintings, human thigh bone trumpets and butter lamps.

After my mother's death I returned temporarily from London to finish the preparations for the final examinations at the university. I moved back into the veranda room; the Tibetan shrine had been transferred to the living-room. My brother and I lived quietly side by side. I had only just begun to grow closer to my mother and during my last visit she had been particularly loving. In the winter months, this dark room lit only by the reading lamp was the right place for study, grief and remorse.

The Bathroom

BATHROOMS in old houses were rare in the sixties in
Austria. Property owners found it too costly to install
new water-pipes and drains. People improvised by
putting bathtubs into kitchens, sometimes under a col-
lapsible counter or in a corner behind a curtain. It
is possible that Mr Körösi, who had Franckstrasse 31
built, had read some of the articles by the Viennese
architect Adolf Loos where he praised the highly developed bathing culture he had encountered in England and in some parts of North America. He thought
of these plumbing wonders as an originally Germanic
achievement and he exhorted the old-fashioned and
water-shy Austrians to invest in proper bathrooms with
running water. At any rate, the Old German-style
house Franckstrasse 31 did have dedicated bathrooms
built into the two largest and best appointed of the flats,
the ones meant to be occupied by more affluent and
enlightened tenants. Those on the mezzanine, the attic
flat and that of the caretakers had not been deemed
worthy of such luxury.

The bathrooms of the large flats were situated on
the western side and the one on the first floor gave on
to a masonry balcony which was accessed through

double doors glazed with leaded windows. During our time, the equipment of the original bathroom only survived on the second floor, which still featured a sunken, though leaking, bathtub of black marble. Our bathroom had been modernized before we moved in. The bath was a freestanding, cast-iron, enamelled tub, long and wide enough for a person to lie fully immersed. There was also a bidet. The white tiles, with their Art Nouveau frieze of pink morning glory on a pale green background, had been damaged wherever alterations had been made.

It was a comfortable bathroom, well-lit and well ventilated, spacious. All its installations, the tub, the wash-basin, the bidet, were solid and well proportioned. The stone mosaic floor was reminiscent of the South, and it was always a particular pleasure to take a bath on a summer's afternoon, looking at the aloes from Croatia that had been planted in the stone bowls on the balcony.

In this bathroom Ferdinand Körösi, who had commissioned the building, was said to have taken his own life. He had apparently been deeply in debt, most likely bankrupt, and ruined by the exorbitant cost of the building-work, he had hung himself in his bathroom.

In the country we had heard of people who had hung themselves in desperation after they had lost their farm, their all, in some card game. This tended to involve the calving rope, and the hanging would have taken place in the hayloft or the stable. Lying in the warm suds I tried to imagine how Mr Körösi would had gone about doing it in this bathroom. I asked myself whether he had fetched the long ladder from the cellar and then climbed to the sturdy pipes that ran horizontally just below the ceiling, or whether he had wound the belt of his dressing gown around his neck; after all it would have been hard to get hold of a calving rope in this neighbourhood. Then, trusting the firmness of the pipe he would have kicked over the ladder and then, later, someone would have found him. These images made the lovely bathroom at first a slightly spooky space but the uncomfortable feeling faded. The unhappy man – whose name I have only recently discovered in the planning department's archive – was forgotten, and the fact that his was the first death in this house and that it had occurred in our bathroom.

The bathroom was a refuge for us half-grown daughters where we could lock ourselves in, each one separately of course, in order to devote ourselves without interruption to our bodies. The scary experience of puberty with all its repulsive signs – the blackheads, the greasy skin, the dandruff, the unexpected growth of hair in strange places, the bleedings – these we were particularly conscious of in the bathroom and we tried to deal with such unpleasant manifestations of irreversible change with applications of almond scrubs, razor blades, black tar soap and similar means. There was something suitably clinical about this white-tiled room, and all traces of these ministrations had to be carefully removed. However, one could have an enjoyable time there too, lying in a deep bath while talking to a girlfriend on the phone; the cable was long enough to put the receiver on a stool next to the tub.

Later, my mother had a shower hose installed in the bath to reduce the usage of water and the time that running a bath required. Taking a shower without flooding the floor was only possible with a certain technique in handling the hose while squatting in the bath. She also bought a wall-mounted, mirrored cabinet. Here one could see one's face from both sides and practice the difficult act of applying eye liner. This cabinet had also a built-in neon light and magnifying mirror, which showed freckles and other blemishes in horrifying detail. The bathroom and its mirrors were witnesses to our gradual transformation from teenagers to women.

In the winter the bathroom was also used to dry clothes. Although there was a drying room in the attic, no servants were available to carry the heavy laundry basket with wet washing all the way up there. So our mother hung the dripping bedlinen on ropes that crisscrossed the bathroom. They hung there like limp rigging through which we had to forge a path to the wash-basin. This damp laundry reminded me of the story of *The One who Went Out to Know Fear*, and his shuddering on feeling the cold wetness of fish across his back.

The Water Closet

JUST WHICH word is used to refer to the room solely dedicated to the evacuation of bladder and bowels to some extent still reveals the social class of the speaker. In English private houses such dedicated rooms are rare, as most bathrooms also contain a toilet, which also allows people to simply ask for the bathroom when needing what the upper classes call 'the lavatory'. Toilets in bathrooms were unheard of in Austria until quite recently, hence the need for a designation. The original contraption, the English invention of the water closet that flushed excreta from a receptacle filled and immediately refilled with water, gave rise to the whole room being referred to as the closet, or just the WC, with German using as loanword *Klosett* or *Klo*.

On the plans for Franckstrasse 31 the architect had labelled the respective spaces in the flats on the mezzanine and the middle floors as C (*closet*), while those for the lower social classes were marked as AB for *Abort*, or privy – a reference to the more primitive outhouses in Austria, mainly built of timber, where human waste fell into a hole that had to be emptied at regular intervals to be used as fertilizer on fields and gardens.

None of the water closets provided in Franckstrasse 31 had facilities for handwashing; a fact typical of the hygienic standards in Austria at the time. The architect wanted to have the toilet accessible from the hallway and he provided ventilation by means of a shaft fitted above the pantry behind the toilet. This shaft could be closed with a glazed frame by means of a wooden handle. In summer this window was left wide open, but in winter it was reduced to a narrow slit which reduced the airflow. The construction of the bowl with its flat receiving surface was further conducive to the development of smells. It therefore made no difference if usage concerned the second-floor water closet of the 'Frau President', as we called the widow of a former post-office president, or that of the caretakers in the basement, as it was always obvious to anyone in the hallway when somebody had just been performing a bowel movement.

The equipment in our flat must have dated from the time the house was built. The iron water cistern was placed very high, just below the ceiling, and was manipulated by means of a wooden handle fastened to the metal chain. The contents of the cistern emptied in one massive gush into the bowl, while the container was noisily refilled. Nearly three metres had to be traversed between the bowl and the door to the hallway and the mighty noise like that of a waterfall at one's back was rather frightening at night. To wash one's hands was not easy, especially in the mornings, when the single bathroom was occupied by siblings and lodgers.

The ventilation shaft, to be found in many of the old buildings in Graz, could also serve as a hiding place. We were told of cases where women and young girls used these shafts to hide from the Russian occupying forces in order to keep from getting raped. When I asked my mother whether the Jews of Graz had also been hiding in such places, she said that all the Jews in Graz had emigrated to Palestine and had no need to hide. The fate of the Jews of Graz did not interest her enough to try and find out what could have happened to those unwilling or unable to emigrate to Palestine. Whenever I think of the toilet in Franckstrasse 31, I am not only reminded of the bad smells and the noisy eruption of water but also of something quite uncanny going on behind one's back.

The Kitchen Maid's Room

WHILE THE CHAMBER beside the entrance to the flat was designated as the sleeping place of a house or parlour maid, the room described on the plan as the maid's room (*Magdkammer*), next to the kitchen and accessible only through the kitchen, was clearly meant for someone working there. This room lay on the eastern side of the bathroom and a single window overlooked the lateral façade of the neighbouring building. It was smaller than the kitchen by a third and smaller than the 12 square metres of the parlour maid's room I inhabited. I only discovered this when I looked at the architect's plans since it was by no means obvious that my narrow room was larger than the wider and shorter chamber next to the kitchen. When our mother had a central heating system installed, the boiler was built into a cupboard against the wall to the bathroom, which made the room even smaller. In this floor-to-ceiling cupboard she stored suitcases, boxes with Christmas decorations, bath towels and unworn winter or summer clothes. A simple sofa-bed fitted snugly into the width of the room on the wall opposite, a bed that had been used by our father as a student. It was covered with a blanket of soft brown velvet. When we had still lived in the country our mother liked to lie down on it after lunch and she loved having my sister and me snuggle down beside her. The pile of the velvet material had the same soft consistency as the skin on my mother's cheeks.

This room was assigned to my sister: she had ended up with the smallest room in the flat but was happy enough to no longer have to share the master's room with our brother. Our mother had bought a wall-mounted shelf unit similar to mine and a hinged table that fitted below the window. It was the only room in the flat where the floor was covered with linoleum though it was brightened by a gaily patterned Bosnian kilim. The gas boiler in the cupboard and the relatively large radiator made this room a warm nest and my sister soon discovered its advantages. She could fetch herself something to snack on during the night, she could lock herself in – and so she put up with the large wicker basket filled with laundry to be ironed that always was put there, as well as with the fact that there was only a little space for her own clothes in the cupboard. She did not feel the confinement of her room. She did not envy me for the my view of the garden. Instead, she was happy to be nearer to our mother who spent most of her time in the kitchen and whose room was only separated from hers by the bathroom.

My sister had been born only 17 months after my birth, a fact that was often mentioned, as if she herself had been impatient, as if she had wanted it that way. This was also a veiled reference to the unreliability of the *Knaus-Ogino* contraceptive method. I only discovered from my aunt, decades after my mother's death, that my father had performed an abortion on my mother before they were married, and that it had been risky from a medical point of view. It is likely that my mother refused to terminate another pregnancy when they realized that fact of her new pregnancy not long after my birth. Their financial situation was precarious at the time, my father had not obtained the necessary contracts with the main medical insurers and his income was therefore very small. My mother must have fought for this child. When the baby was born it failed to thrive and screamed in pain until it was discovered that she suffered from milk intolerance. As soon as the food was adjusted, the infant recovered and she was so pretty that everybody was pleased with her. She had our father's large brown eyes, her hair was curly and abundant and her skin had a light golden tinge. While I had always wanted to be a father's child and sunned myself in the glory of his approval of me, my sister was a mother's child, finding herself particularly comforted by the warmth of the mother's embrace. My existence as the elder sister, always a few steps ahead, was a fact she resented, especially as I had little patience for her inability to keep up with me. I began to talk at an early age but she found little reason to say anything herself.

I climbed trees and ran like a weasel: she was content to watch me do so. Since she had no interest to rival me in areas where I wished to shine, we discovered other mutual interests, where we were as one heart and as one soul. There were certain games she invented that had no specific rules but plenty of repetitions of certain words and gestures. The time we spent together in England without our brother, who was then still a baby, strengthened our bond even more. I missed her terribly when she had to spend some weeks in hospital after she caught scarlet fever but she was proud of her time there and of the fact that she had managed without me. As she was by nature confiding and trusting, I considered her too easily taken advantage of and saw it as my duty to disabuse her of such naïve confidence. I did not succeed. She insisted on the pretty images she had constructed in her head and she rejected my disbelief as cynicism. My desire to protect her and to protect her from herself became even more urgent after our father's death. During the first dark months we spent at boarding school, we formed a united front against a strange and hostile world represented by the nuns.

In this former kitchen maid's room my sister spent the last years of her childhood, still playing with dolls and her doll's pram. There she spent her adolescence, then her early adulthood. She incubated herself in this nest, the smallest and most inconspicuous room in the flat. During puberty, between her twelfth and the fifteenth year, the difference in age between us sisters became very noticeable – as this younger sibling reacted with violent emotion to the fact that her elder sister was changing into someone she no longer recognized, someone who did not wish to spend time with somebody as childish as she was still. She was furious when she found me snogging the young Serb on the Croatian island and outraged that our mother did not punish such behaviour. When I was allowed to go to London on my own, to visit our aunt there, she was justifiably resentful. She also hated me for my quarrels with our mother. She hated herself and her looks; her formerly beautiful hair became rough and wiry and the mirror showed her only a scowling, dissatisfied face. My sister was a much prettier child than I had ever been; nobody paid me compliments for my looks – only perhaps for my intelligence or my strength – but my sister was lovely to behold. Although she was quite as intelligent as I was, she mainly received praise for her curls, her large eyes and her cuddly ways. While I steadily trained my boyish body so that my broad shoulders grew even broader and my muscles firmer, she put up no defences against the changes brought on by puberty. An inborn curvature of the lower spine made running and exercises painful and so she could not sublimate her adolescence by training. What Freud called the *most significant but also the most painful task* of puberty, the separation from one's parents, was much harder for her because she persisted in her childhood love for our mother and she turned her hatred against me, the older sister who always knew better. She locked herself into her chamber where she stored up her fury until she erupted from her door, falling upon me with her fists and showing a strength I had never suspected.

This hatred against me and the disgust she felt for herself slowly abated and came to an end with her defloration. Her first boyfriend was a friend of my first boyfriend and like him an adult, ten years older. My mother was fond of him despite the dungarees he liked to wear and his long hair, because she had a high regard for his mother, a well-known Nazi poet.

Now there was no longer any need to be envious or resentful of me. For a while we even found it amusing to become hard to tell apart. Her hair was then as short as mine, we dressed in the same way in trousers or mini-skirts, wore the same style of make-up and appeared at parties as an entertaining pair of sisters. She had little understanding of my mania for hitchhiking and my attempts at running away but shared my interest in trying out the various consciousness-altering substances, the drugs our mother was so afraid we would get addicted to. She shared my enthusiasm for the improvised jazz that could be heard every night in a basement of the music academy as well as my interest in art exhibitions and the events at the Forum Stadtpark. She took part in the happenings that occurred more or less spontaneously across the city and the drunken parties that the architecture students organized in the vineyards, and she came with me and my friends to see films by Fellini, Bergman, Godard, Truffaut and Altmann.

Unlike me, she never antagonized her teachers and was never in danger of having to repeat a year. She passed her *Matura* before me and when she announced that she did not intend to study in Graz but in Paris, it came as a complete surprise to our mother, who had not reckoned with such a show of independence from her younger daughter. Her departure for Paris marked the completion of the *painful psychic task* of puberty and her emancipation from her sister.

The Kitchen

THE PRODUCTIVE spaces of the flats in Franckstrasse 31 were situated at the far corner of the flats that overlooked the garden. This contained the kitchen maid's chamber, the kitchen, the pantry and the kitchen balcony. The smaller flats on the mezzanine and attic lacked maids' rooms because there the housewife was expected to do without a live-in help.

The kitchens in the city were very different from the ones we had been used to in the country. The farmhouse kitchens were not only places where the various products of the farm were turned into food, but each was the centre of the farm's social life, where the daily meals were taken together and where seasonal celebrations took place. In a bourgeois household, however, staff in the kitchen prepared the meals the family consumed in the dining-room. My paternal grandmother had never set foot in the kitchen and had never, during her long life, cooked a single meal. When she gave up her household she either lived with one of the daughters who looked after her or took her meals in restaurants.

The original fittings of a kitchen in the large flats were by the time we came, only preserved on the second floor. This had been furnished with the latest equipment available around 1900: a built-in range, called a 'kitchen machine', heated with coal and gas. Concentric rings let into the cast-iron hotplate allowed for instant variations in temperature and several water-basins provided hot water. There were also different-sized ovens. The walls were covered in easy-to-clean white tiles, the floor with wood cement, and the cupboards painted in white gloss.

Our kitchen had been converted and modernized by previous tenants. A free-standing electric hob with four hot plates and a single oven had replaced the range. Next to it was the sink. A rectangular kitchen table, a corner bench and two chairs stood in the corner next to my sister's room. Dirty linen was kept in the hollow spaces of the benches, to be washed in the machine that stood between the balcony door and the pantry.

We took all our meals at this corner table. A set of cupboards on either side served to store the kitchen utensils, the plates, dishes and provisions. Some were wall-mounted and some standing on the floor to provide work surfaces. All the wood was painted a lime-green gloss. None of the units were built in. The large refrigerator, the hob and the washing machine all stood as separate objects. The red wood-cement floor showed every step and had to be polished at least once a week. Light came through the glazed balcony door that was always open in the summer. As in the bathroom, laundry was hung there on ropes to dry.

When we still lived in the country, our mother was able to play a professional if unremunerated role in the surgery. She wore a white coat like my father and assisted him in minor surgical interventions, counselled patients, dressed wounds, supervised the store of medicines and did all the accounts. She had a live-in helper who took care of most of the household chores and the cooking so that she spent little time in the small kitchen we had there. After our father's death our mother became a full-time housewife in sole charge of the modernized kitchen in Franckstrasse 31. She tried to make the room more cosy by hanging framed photographs of happier times on the walls, as well as some old stoneware plates from the Herdergasse villa. She fastened cushions to the hard kitchen chairs, hung net curtains on the windows and made sure that the kitchen was always in good order. The dishes were washed and tidied away after every meal, a task that we girls had to help with. I never minded doing housework, I quite liked doing it, but my sister showed no enthusiasm for this and my brother was never even asked.

My mother had attended cookery classes before she had got married and she always followed the repertoire of dishes she learnt to cook there. The recipe book published by the nun who ran the classes was the only one she ever consulted. She used to cater for the culinary preferences of her husband who insisted on his daily beef broth soup, a meat dish with sautéed potatoes and a large bowl of green lettuce. She became an excellent soup cook; not only her beef broth made of bones, root vegetables and fresh meat, but her vegetable soups were also superb, and I cannot say that I ever managed to cook a vegetable soup as delicious as the ones she prepared. The schnitzel, the roast chicken, the goulash, were all of reliable quality, only when it came to vegetables did she fall back into old Austrian habits of binding everything in a flour *roux*. She cooked with butter and lard, used oil only for salads, adding in the summer plenty of fresh herbs – parsley, dill and thyme. She prepared the food in a systematic manner, always rinsing the used dishes and wiping the surfaces between the different stages of preparation. Some of the dishes required considerable labour, such as the stuffed peppers, where the rice, the peppers, the tomato sauce all had to be cooked separately, the boiled tomatoes having to be pressed through a sieve and thickened with a light *roux*.

Her own preference was for warm desserts, which she liked to make us for supper – rice puddings, pancakes, soufflés, bread and butter puddings and the semolina gruel we all loathed. We children preferred cold collations, cold boiled beef with vinegar and oil, but she insisted that we should have something warm and rich in calories before going to bed. For breakfast we had fresh white rolls that the grocer delivered every morning, with hot chocolate for us and tea with milk for her. Tea was also drunk in the afternoon, with a sandwich. Coffee was only prepared for visitors. There was hardly ever any cake. Biscuits were made only for Christmas.

Sometimes her own mother came – to prepare an *Apfelstrudel*. Her mother was a good though slovenly cook. Oma's *Apfelstrudel* entailed an enormous effort and the use of almost every single utensil in the kitchen. The dough, of flour, water and vegetable oil, had to be kneaded on the special wooden board for a long while, and had to be banged hard on the surface to make the dough elastic enough to be pulled into transparent sheets, and, spread over an old table-cloth, it almost touched the floor. She took the peeled and thinly sliced apples that she spread on a third of this to the dough that was liberally coated with warm butter. Then she added the breadcrumbs that had been toasted in butter and then, with a priest-like gesture, she plunged her hand deep into the sugar bowl to sprinkle the coarse crystal sugar from on high, in a sacrificial as well as prodigal gesture, followed by a powdering of cinnamon, before she lifted the cloth on the side with the fruit and breadcrumbs so that a large roll, the width of arm, emerged, that was bent into a U-shape and placed in a large, buttered roasting-pan. This thick roll was then glazed with a beaten egg and put in the pre-heated oven. Our grandmother then had a rest, while her kitchen helpers tried to convert the chaos into the customary order. The large Austrian ravioli, filled with potatoes, mint and fresh curds, demanded a similar effort and this was also worth it.

Our mother was not a nervous person but Oma's performance in her kitchen made her nervous and irritable, which in turn provoked her mother's malice so as to make her even more irritable. She wanted to see at what point her daughter would crack. Most of the time, she could control herself but at times there was a fight, bad things were said, until Oma went away, half-satisfied, half-resentful, and weeks had to pass before she was asked to come again. Then she turned up, proffered a *Guglhupf*, and peace was restored for a while.

Oma also did the ironing, a task my mother abhorred. Even so she insisted that every sheet, napkin and handkerchief had to be ironed, every tea towel, and that the linen cupboards were kept immaculate. Oma ironed on the kitchen table on layers of old blankets and sheets, pressing the laundry pieces she had previously sprinkled with water. Afterwards she played cards with us, or Ludo, a game which allows good insights into the good will or malice of each player.

The corner table was not only a place to eat, to do the ironing, and to prepare complicated dishes that needed more space than the usual worktop. It was also a place to sit down when one was tired of one's own room, or to read the newspaper, and it was also a neutral place of conviviality, for playing cards, or simply for sitting together. Especially after lunch, the dishes dried, order re-established, our mother liked to sit there with us. We talked about school, complained about unjust treatment by the teachers or rejoiced over successful examinations; I sometimes allowed myself to comment on a lesson that I found particularly interesting or expand upon some detail, which bored the others. For a while one of the lodgers joined us and his sarcasm goaded our adolescent insecurities, but there were hours when he played Hans Baumann songs on his recorder; Baumann being a composer who had written some of the most popular tunes during the Nazi era. My mother had sung these songs at the Nazi youth gatherings and we even learned them in our convent school, since the education ministry found them fit for inclusion in the authorized Second Republic song-books. We sat around the table, singing these songs and rather relished singing them; the tunes were catchy and the lyrics about the dawn breaking, about marching on country roads and bringing in the harvest. These were the last hours of familial unity, as were the hours during Advent, when we made stars of flattened straw for the Christmas tree.

The kitchen could also be a place of combat, not necessarily physical, where accusations, insults, blame and outrage were traded, not only between the siblings, especially between me and my sister – who stoked her fury in her chamber next door and then suddenly exploded – but between my mother and me.

I had gradually come to some understanding about the last war and the crimes of National Socialism. This period of history could not be discussed at school but it was possible to get some information if one wanted to. Our mother defended her continuing allegiance to the *Führer*. For her, the pictures of concentration camps were nothing but Hollywood propaganda. The Jews had all emigrated to Palestine long before, and to have locked up and killed invalids and communists had not been that deplorable; after all, there had been a war going on and it was more important to ensure that the healthy people survived, and the communists would have betrayed Germany to the Russians. I defended the communists and declared that only a new communist revolution could save us from a third and final world war. Furthermore, I was all in favour of the Cultural Revolution and of Mao-tse-tung; that was just what we needed in Austria and especially in Graz. My mother said that I had no idea how bad it had been before the war and what a relief it had been when Austria became part of the *Reich*. Everybody thought so, she herself had cheered the *Führer*; the town square had been overflowing with people bursting with excitement. I could not even imagine the enthusiasm.

These quarrels did not amount to discussions, they were violent clashes between generations and ideologies. I came to see my mother more and more as an old Nazi, one who was even proud of it and one who did not try to dissimulate that fact like so many other old Nazis. To a degree I even respected her for this stance – of not denying her old allegiance, of having the courage to defend the beliefs she had formed in her youth at a time, during our Second Republic, when it was only possible to speak about this among like-minded people. On the other hand I found it intolerable that she should be, if no longer enthusiastic, still a loyal follower of the *Führer*, whom she never referred to by name. It was her way of honouring him. She also never forget to remind us on the 20th of April that it was his birthday.

She in turn detested the long-haired boys, the hippies, the work-shy, dirty, drug-addicted, communist seducers of 'today's youth', who had already got hold of me and my sister, which inevitably meant that we would end up in the gutter. How our father would beat us if he were still alive; how I dragged everything down with my cynicism and my arrogance, when I had no idea about life or anything. Then I would slam the kitchen door behind me and she would sit there and cry in desperation because she did not know what to do with me. She threatened to have me consigned to the notorious correction facility for fallen girls that was run by some nuns; they would show me.

We sang no more Baumann songs. I moved out of the flat and my mother gave up trying to keep me on the straight and narrow. At times, when I came on a visit and we sat in the kitchen corner or went for a walk together, we avoided all contentious subjects and I noticed in myself an almost childish tenderness for her when she was close to me, a tenderness I sorely missed after her death, when I sat in the kitchen on my own, sadly, thinking of all the battles we had fought there and of the good times too.

The Pantry

AT THE BACK of the building there were small window openings next to the kitchen balconies between the projecting part housing the stairwell and the balcony. Above that were even smaller, hatch-like openings. These small windows belonged to the pantries, which, according to the plans, were built into the extension of the space occupied by the toilets; an axis of digestion where the food kept in the pantry ended up being evacuated just behind the wall. In the seventies and later on, the occupants of the mezzanine, basement and attic flats were to sacrifice their useful pantry to have a small bathroom installed there.

Whenever we children were feeling peckish, we would look into the pantry to see if there were any remains of meals. There was always a loaf of dark rye bread and a large pot of rendered lard. We were allowed to help ourselves to bread and lard, while our mother discouraged us from taking the more precious salami or cheese from the fridge without asking first. The pantry lay in the shade of the projecting stairwell and towards the north. The small window had wooden shutters that could be closed in the summer and so this was a cool room, suitable for keeping food fresh. The pantry, like the linen cupboard, was a place to demonstrate the virtues of a housewife. Stacks of starched, pressed bed-linen demonstrated at least the conscientious house-wife's control of staff, as well as the degree to which she had internalized prevailing notions of order and clean-liness. However, it was only the housewife herself who was proud or ashamed of the state of her linen cup-board, since who else from outside the members of the household had access to it? The pantry was far more accessible. One could ask a visitor to select one of the preserves that were kept there. My aunt's pantry was exemplary in all respects. On wooden shelves were rows of Kilner jars and pots, arranged by size and colour, their contents identified on neatly written labels. There were jams and confitures of apricots, peaches, plums, currants, strawberries, raspberries, stewed compotes of cherries, apricots, white peaches, but also fine vegetables: asparagus, green beans, young peas, tiny carrots, as well as wild mushrooms in oil, which I coveted most. Only rarely, when the aunt was in an unusually good mood, would she let us have one of the little jars filled with small *cèpes*. Below those shelves stood ranks of bottles filled with thickened raspberry or currant cordial.

In 1955, when my sister and I spent some months in London, we were particularly impressed with our London aunt's pantry. Instead of the home-made jams, stewed fruit and fine vegetables, there were tins made in factories with their colourful labels – American cling peaches in thick syrup, peeled slices of mandarins, fruit salad, rounds of pineapples, and, in addition, tins with cooked beans, lentils, peeled tomatoes, also meat and fish conserves – corned beef, ham, tuna chunks. The pantries of my two aunts revealed two different worlds and periods, differences that the other rooms of their dwellings did not make as obvious. The pantry of the aunt in Bergmanngasse was always well-stocked because she lived alone and her household consisted only of her and her dog, for whom she cooked a full meal every day. The tins of the London aunt were as much a sign of the food shortages after the First and the Second World War as the glass jars of my Graz aunt, only less concerned with proving housewifely labour, less virtuous and hence more modern, relying on mass-produced goods.

Our pantry was one of a reluctant housewife, since our mother had freed herself early from the *petit bourgeois* ideals of her own mother and had learned not just one but three different professions in order to stand on her own feet, as she said, and not be left at the mercy of a man to support her. She had always worked and had chosen a husband at whose side she was able to function in a professional capacity, while she delegated the housework to a paid help. After our father's death we lived off the medical association's contributions to orphans and the interest of the inheritance that was administered in the United States. It proved impossible for our mother to find employment that would have paid enough to afford the fees for the private education that was deemed fitting for our social standing and for the salary of a housekeeper. So she became a housewife, although she never indicated this as her profession, always insisting on writing 'physician's widow' on any forms. This reluctant housewife managed her household well enough, given her general competence and intelligence, as well as her abhorrence of chaos and disorder.

The pantry, however, showed the limits of her ambition: although the mandatory ranks of jam jars were on the shelves, most of them were mouldy. There were a few tins of the sort of food we children liked – ravioli, sardines, fruit salad – and these were served only on special occasions. As long as the trees in the garden bore fruit, she made compotes of stewed apricots and peaches. Once on a whim she bought a manual press to turn the apples from the garden into juice, a most laborious process, where the apples had to be washed, cut into pieces and liquidized in an electric mixer before being squeezed by the press that the lodger operated. The resultant juice than had to be sterilized. It was delicious. The following year she tried to make cider that was kept in a small wooden barrel in the pantry and it produced a very good vinegar. Instead of pickling the mushrooms we had picked in the forest, she dried them in the sun or a low oven and stuffed them into old nylon stockings that she hung in the pantry, where it therefore always smelled faintly of the woody forest humus, as well as of stale wine, given that the empty white wine bottles were also stored there.

The aunt from Bergmanngasse always scrutinized our pantry with critical eyes: the sparsely-filled shelves, the half-heartedly preserved jams and compotes. Our mother, who had also experienced hunger after the Second World War, never succumbed to the impulse to hoard food, food that might have to be thrown away. She made sure that there was always enough fat in the form of lard, enough black bread and potatoes. None of us children shared our mother's predilection for the sweet, warm, milk-based dishes in the Austrian repertoire. We preferred simple boiled potatoes with butter, or potato goulash, as well as my father's favourite, a concoction of potatoes, boiled pasta and onions. When a large jar with sweet-sour pickled gherkins happened to be kept in the pantry, I would often meet one of the siblings there, since we hankered after pickles and all things sour. Best of all we liked a dish composed of layers of sliced boiled potatoes, chopped ham, sliced hard boiled eggs, all covered with a thick layer of sour cream and baked in the oven. It was particularly delicious cold, surreptitiously eaten right there, in the pantry.

On the Second Floor

ON THE SECOND floor lived the widow of a former post-office president, who was known in the house as 'Frau President'. She comported herself in a suitably dignified manner, walked with measured steps, assisted by a cane. She wore closely-fitted garments and was trussed up in tightly belted coats that enclosed her thickset body like armour. She favoured cloche hats, drawn low onto her brow above a heavily powdered, fleshy face. I never saw Frau President smile; at most she gave a slight and condescending nod when greeted. She never exchanged a word with the other inhabitants of the house and never seemed to receive visitors.

The most remarkable thing about this person was the odour she emitted. While the room and the clothes of the Little Woman in the basement spread the beast-like reek of rural poverty, the appearance of Frau President in the communal stairway left behind the exquisite scent of expensive perfume. It had to be Parma Violets that she used to sprinkle on her massive body, and I wondered how many thousands of these fragile flowers must have been extracted to achieve a saturation strong enough to cause it to linger for a long while after she had gone. We children loved to hold the glazed swing-door open for her when Frau President approached in her customary measured pace and, as she passed by, we inhaled, deeply.

In contrast to the tenants inhabiting the apartments below us, she never complained about noise. That would have been beneath her dignity. She preferred to maintain her distance. She lived alone in her large flat with its suite of rooms and the bay window. Occasionally she received a visit from her son, whose bent-over way of walking suggested a long habit of subservience. After his mother's death he moved into her flat and then we heard, with some astonishment, that this meek and middle-aged man had got married. No doubt his mother would never have permitted that during her lifetime. We referred to his wife, with some irony, as the young Frau President. In no way did she resemble her mother-in-law – she was certainly not young – but in whose environment, since nothing could be changed, she was now condemned to live.

This person, Frau R., sought out my sister, who remained in the flat after our mother's death, to be her ally in the long-lasting battles with the owners of the house, who tried their utmost to force out the two women occupying the best flats in the building. This meant that my sister came to know the second-floor flat that I never saw. It had, so she said, preserved the original fittings from the time the house was built. The furniture was all in the Art Nouveau style, and the bathroom still had the now leaky, sunken, black marble bath. The kitchen too was like something to be found in a museum of interiors, with its large built-in range and polished copper water-basins. My sister was particularly taken by the veranda, filled with ferns and luscious evergreens, interspersed with delicate cane furniture, as in a tropical hotel.

Here lived the young Frau President, widowed soon after marriage, in the atmosphere of her mother-in-law, an atmosphere which in turn preserved that of the time when the original Frau President was first betrothed. After several decades, the owners succeeded in getting hold of this Art Nouveau specimen of a flat, and duly had it trivialized according to the exigencies of modern life.

The Attic Storey

UNLIKE IN PARIS, where impoverished tenants occupied unheated, shabby rooms under the eaves, the desire to make a profit from the attic spaces of newly built tenements was not widespread in Graz during its Belle Époque. The attic spaces there served to store old furniture and boxes, as well as a place to dry laundry. Whether Herr Körösi, who owned Franckstrasse 31, was inspired by the Parisian examples cannot be known, but he did decide to have two flats built into the attic. According to the first drawings of the architect, he had planned three differently formed roofs, each ornamented with artful gable decorations, under which two flats were to be fitted, each composed of two rooms, a kitchen, a balcony, a hallway and pantry; and one lavatory to be shared by both households. In the space between them he made room for a generally accessible attic room for storage. Clearly, the flats were intended to be respectable flats for small families or couples, not mere garrets. In the end a simpler roof structure was decided upon but the two flats remained, one on each side of the communal attic.

When we moved in, only one of the flats was occupied. Here lived the elderly widow of a privy counsellor,

Frau W. While the Little Woman lived close to the earth in the basement, Frau W. dwelt like a swallow under the eaves. Her fragile body, her very movements, had something birdlike about them. She was the oldest person in the house and it was hard for her to climb the three storeys. She always wore black clothes, made of brittle, shiny materials and laced ankle-boots. My sister and I sometimes offered to carry her net bag with shopping for her when we happened to meet her in the stairs. She thanked us by offering us a glass of raspberry cordial, while inviting us to be seated, not in her little kitchen but in her salon.

Under the inclined eaves the space unfolded like a doll's house cut from paper. Lace curtains, fastened onto the window panes by brass rods, filtered light and shadows so that this room seemed remote from the world. The light blond Biedermeier furniture, the little chests of drawers, the delicate round tables and fragile chairs were as fragile and fine as Mrs W. herself. Although she was a widow it was impossible to imagine any man inhabiting these rooms. We were particularly enchanted by the many silhouettes cut from black paper that she had hung in golden frames on her walls. She would point to them – this was a sister, that a cousin, and this had once been herself.

She seemed to have lived in these rooms, so high above the pavement of Franckstrasse, in the everlasting paper-cut world of her maidenhood, her Biedermeier youth – and she had retained a youthful gracefulness. We were only too aware of our coarseness and how careful we had to be with her thin wafer-thin porcelain cups, the wobbly lyre-backed chairs. We never stayed long, fearing that just one careless movement would cause it all to break apart.

Our voices, so she told my mother when they met in the stairwell, were like bird song to her ears, our screams in the gardens were delightful to her. But we were too preoccupied with each other and with ourselves to notice when and how Frau W. disappeared from her airy attic flat.

The Attic

THE ROOFS of the old city of Graz can be seen to best advantage from the Schlossberg, the rock in the middle of the city that once housed the fortified castle before Napoleon insisted on its demolition after his victory over the Austrians at Wagram.

From the clock-tower, one of the two surviving medieval monuments, there's a good view over the closely spaced terraced buildings with their red tiled roofs, which, like the scaly backs of great beasts, wind along the narrow streets of the old city. The roofs of houses built close to the mountain nearly touch it and for a while it was indeed possible to get access through one of the gardens at the lower part of the Schlossberg, and to penetrate these great long attics which united all those of the individual houses in one huge space. Little gaps in the tiles admitted shafts of light and our footsteps made the dust from the old floor-boards rise up in snow-like clouds.

In the attic of Franckstrasse 31 the washing lines still criss-crossed the dimly lit space, but only long cobwebs hung there. There were two small windows and we could see some old chests, cupboards and trunks standing singly or in groups as on a stage, until they too disappeared one day in a practical clearance.

It was less mysterious to be in this attic than in those of the old houses in the old city. The building was too new, but it did remind me of the haylofts in the country at the end of winter when the hay had all been used up. Then the beams, the thick planks and the whole structure that carried the roof became clearly visible. They all seemed so solid and lasting, something lifted well away from the dampness of the earth, in a silence in which time itself became dust.